KINGDOM OF CAIN

Tanner Hnidey

Kingdom of Cain

by

Tanner Hnidey

ISBN: 978-1-7382773-0-8

Independently Published

First Edition

For Paige

Contents

CHAPTER 1

The Kingdom of Choice

The old proverbs say, "If it looks like a duck, swims like a duck, and quacks like a duck, it's probably a duck." The new proverbs say, "If it has a deep voice like a man, an Adam's apple like a man, and male chromosomes like a man, he's possibly a female." As for myself, I prefer proverbs that teach, "If it applauds progressivism, promises progressivism, and advances progressivism, it's probably poison."

Modern men and women don't justify their beliefs on grounds of objective reason, law, or nature, but on grounds of subjective sentiments like emotion, desire, and pleasure. A man tells the world he wants to be himself, but then proceeds to commit pseudo suicide as he turns into someone totally unrecognizable and foreign to himself. While he proclaims with pride, "I am who I am," by artificially transitioning to a female gender, he proves "I am" is exactly who he doesn't want to be. Though he was born a male and looks like a male, he believes he's a woman, and in his totalitarianism, demands we affirm it to be so.

As examples like these become more common in society, we need to start christening every newborn with the phrase, "Welcome to our world, where *everyone does what's right in their own eyes*" (Judges 17:6). Of course, doing so assumes we still have newborns to christen. We pride ourselves in the fact that we don't commit the sins of Carthage and offer child sacrifices to a pagan god, but we do. We're a more industrious machine of child sacrifice than any society which has come before us. A woman demands an abortion, calling it a justified human right, because she's a "single, independent, woman, and not a mother." Her stomach protrudes, and a precious human being develops inside her, but she has no tolerance for a child, so childless she shall be.

Modern medicine has blessed us with the ability to save many lives, but it's also cursed us with the ability to terminate many more. Using these innovations, political successors of Ahab, and spiritual offspring of Jezebel, like Justin Trudeau, Nancy Pelosi, and Alexandria Ocasio-Cortez, unveil a depraved Moloch on the steps of government, and flood their hallowed halls with the crimson blood of babies. This ferocious beast has an insatiable appetite for slaughter, and our leaders feed his hunger every day. They don't just worship the god of abortion, they're his dedicated priests, and vessels of incarnation.

It's uncomfortable to think that such genocide is happening right here at home, so we push it out of our thoughts. Moderate men tolerate extreme things and muse that procedures such as abortion are disagreeable, but unavoidable. "Out of sight, out of mind" they say to themselves. But the child in the womb does see. He sees a weapon of annihilation right before it purges his sight and silences his mind.

Granted, many men and women have also silenced their minds, preferring instead to listen to their feelings. The ancients believed in following a code of justice, whether inscribed by Hammurabi, Moses, or Justinian, but current ideologues believe themselves to be the code. As far as activists are concerned, they don't need to submit to justice, because they believe they *are* justice. Consequently, their actions are hideously unjust.

In a court of law, opposing sides argue back and forth about morality, until a consensus is reached. But in the case of abortion, the defence—the child—is left defenceless and voiceless. Activists slip the charge of genocide by refusing to acknowledge that babies are human in the womb. There's nothing convincing or intellectual about their argument. What else could the child in the womb be if not a human? A dog? A cat? A computer? "A clump of cells" or a "fetus" is a more common response, but it's every bit as unsatisfactory as all the other answers.

The question isn't whether the baby in the womb is a clump of cells because we're all "clumps of cells," but whether the "clump of cells" growing in the womb is a human clump of cells. Indeed, it is. There's nothing magic about a birth canal. There isn't a particular moment during the gestation period when we can say, "There! Now the 'thing' growing inside its mother is human." Age doesn't determine a man's level of humanity, and neither does his ability, intellect, or level of dependency on others. Even if activists refuse to acknowledge this fact, everyone intuitively knows it's true. There's a reason babies are aborted in the soundless vacuum of the womb: a newborn child's cry is a more powerful and elegant argument for life than anything philosophers and lawyers have ever composed.

The more we listen to the catalogue of arguments in favour of abortion, the more we realize society justifies it almost exclusively on the grounds of, "protecting, upholding, and guaranteeing, a woman's right to choose." We don't hear people say, "Abortion protects a woman's right to choose, *and no one else is harmed*," and we don't hear, "Abortion protects a woman's right to choose, *and no one's life is lost*." Instead, we hear, "Abortion protects a woman's right to choose, so it has to be legal; it protects her right to choose, so we can never take abortion away." Perhaps our society should also legalize sexual or physical assault on the grounds that it "protects a man's right to choose," as well. Maybe we should legalize everything, considering almost everything we do is the product of self-interested choice.

Because they defend abortion on the grounds of it being "pro-choice," it's acceptable to assume that activists want to live in a world where they're free to make their own decisions. Regrettably, they neglect the fact that freedom is the first thing to die in a world of totally free choice. A society that does whatever it wants in the name of freedom is a society where no one has any freedom. To be freed from all limitation is to be chained up like a rabid dog.

This concept of freedom and limitation is difficult to understand, but the game of hockey offers some help. It's a fast-moving, rough, intense, sport to play. Skaters move on the ice at incredible speeds, and players strategically "check" each other for control of a little rubberized disc called a "puck."

It doesn't take long to understand that the only reason players are able to play hockey, and the only reason fans are able to watch them play, is because barriers of boards and glass separate the ice rink from the spectator's stands. Players are only able to play because the boards keep them from skating off the ice onto concrete. Fans are only able to watch because the glass keeps them from being hit with pucks, bodies, and sticks. Thus, it's not like removing the barriers makes the game more dangerous, it's that removing the barriers removes the game.

Post-modern ideologues probably conclude the boundaries are oppressive, restricting players from playing to their full potential. But the idea that hockey boards restrict the players' freedom is wrong. The barriers aren't restrictive or oppressive. Rather, they're emancipating, and they let us play hockey as it's meant to be played. If we take the boundaries off the ice, we shut ourselves out of the game. Without boards and glass around the ice, no one plays or watches hockey, because the risk of injury to both parties is too serious to tolerate.

It's important to note that the presence or absence of barriers around a rink have no real effect on a player's freedom to step onto the ice. Regarding the size of the rink, rules of the game, and velocities of the shots, the barriers are inert. However, if they aren't present, players choose not to play, because they're worried about potential disaster. Removing the barriers from the ice means players self-restrict their freedom to a greater degree than the boundaries ever did.

Likewise, human beings are granted a permitter to play this game we call "life." We're able to play because we have foundational rules and laws, like boundaries in a rink, telling us what we can and can't do. We're able to trade with each other, because the law says, "You shall not steal" (Exodus 20:15). We're able to have coffee with our neighbours because the law says, "You shall not murder" (Exodus 20:13). We're able to love, because the law says, "You shall not commit adultery" (Exodus 20:14).

Our society can remove these moral laws if it pleases, but doing so doesn't mean people live life to a larger capacity. Instead, it means people cease to live, both literally, and metaphorically, as they huddle in their homes for fear of being caught in the lawlessness of the streets.

Eliminating our moral restrictions in society doesn't mean we're freer to act human; it means we cease to act like humans. The murderer rejects the law of life and steals the lives of others. Adulterers see each other on the street, disregard the laws of marriage, and destroy each other's families. A human understands he can't eat a piece of a fruit from a tree in the middle of a garden, so he is a human. He disobeys the law, eats the fruit, and humanity slips outside of his grasp.

Returning to the problem of choice, abortionists charge forward in their crusade. It's ironic that they champion the right of everyone to choose, considering they deny that right to the baby. Worshipping abortion on the grounds that it manifests a woman's right to choose is really the praise of volition and worship of one's own will. Like everyone else, our lawmakers (who seem to exclusively destroy law), say, "Abortion must be protected because a woman's right to choose must be protected." They defend the choice of abortion, not because it's objectively moral, but because it's objectively a choice. They might as well defend theft because thieves *choose* to steal.

If abortion's justified because it's the exercise of choice, then choice must be our standard of right and wrong. In that case, every action in society immediately becomes moral. The bank robber becomes as righteous as the beggar. In a world where choice is the moral standard, all actions must be permitted, because all actions are products of choice.

It means the young child who chooses to hit his brother is no more or less justified than his sister who chose not to do so. Their parents can't congratulate one child and reprimand the other. Both choices are congratulable because both choices *are* choices.

It also means the judge who drinks a cup of coffee is no more or less legal than the man who assaults his neighbour in the middle of the night. Society can't throw one man behind bars, and have the other man hand out the sentence. Both choices are equally just, again, because both choices are choices.

If a choice is moral simply because it's a choice, no choice can ever be called immoral. If an action is good purely because it's the product of choice, who cares what action you choose? From a moral standpoint, it makes no difference whether you choose to murder your fiancé or marry him. Because both choices are exactly that—choices—they're equally moral.

Thus, living in a world where choice is the standard of right and wrong means living in a world where Adam and Eve never fell, the tyrants of old committed no atrocities, ruthless slavers were not wicked men, and the abortionists of today aren't engaged in a massacre.

But the abortionists of today *are* engaged in a massacre. They're active participants in the massacre of babies, true, but in a twist of irony, these pro-choice ideologues are also massacring choice. The worship of choice is the abortion of choice. Activists eat their dogmas alive. Their worship of personal will murders personal will. The "pro-choice" world they so fervently pursue turns out to be one where no one has any choice, at all.

Like Mr. G.K. Chesterton said, "You cannot admire will in general, because the essence of will is that it is particular."[1] By choosing to worship choice and make it the god they serve, radicals remove the ability to choose anything else to worship. How can they criticize us when we choose to worship something other than choice? Doing so rebels against their religion that says choice is the superior standard of morality.

Regardless, that's exactly what the activists do. They're furious when someone *chooses* to try and block their abortion legislation in court, because it denies their choice to abort a child. When they parade on Parliament Hill, or march down the streets of Washington D.C., they carry pro-choice signs, and on those pro-choice signs are the words, "I'm pro-choice!" or, "My body, my choice!"

But for the front of every sign we immediately see, there exists a backside that remains hidden. While the front of the sign might say, "Give me the right to choose," the back of the sign says something ominous, like, "No one shall *choose* to come against me. I will choose an abortion, and you will not choose to stop me."

Like so many other virtue-signalling, post-modern, perceptions of life, no one *really* believes that choice is the standard of right and wrong. For example:

- We care whether a criminal *chooses* to assault our spouse.
- We care whether a dictator *chooses* to commit genocide.

[1] G.K. Chesterton, Orthodoxy, (Elizabethton: Lumen, 2013), 43.

- We care whether our sibling *chooses* to starve himself.
- We care whether a mother *chooses* to self-harm.
- We care whether a man *chooses* to drink and drive.
- We care whether the court *chooses* to care about such things.

We care about these choices, because certain actions are self-evidently more moral than other actions. Thus, our society shouldn't be pro-choice, but instead, **pro-right choice**. Our desire shouldn't just be to choose, but to choose correctly according to a standard of morals, values, and laws.

Choice alone is insufficient to justify one's actions. We can't say, "Caesar is crucifying Christians" and then assert it's morally acceptable to do so because it's Caesar's choice. Likewise, we can't say, "Justin is using drugs," and then conclude drugs are the moral thing for Justin to do, because he's choosing to do them. Obviously, abortion's the same. We can't say that someone's choosing to have an abortion, and then act like it's moral for them to do so simply because it's a choice.

Granted, this fact about choice and moral justification goes both ways. Just as it's incorrect to say, "Caesar's crucifying Christians" and automatically assume it's moral for him to do so, it's also incorrect to say, "Caesar's crucifying Christians" and automatically assume it's *immoral* for him to do so. Choices aren't inherently good because they're choices, but neither are they inherently evil because they're choices. In every conscious decision, unless you appeal to an objective moral law transcending mankind, no one can say anything about the objective morality of any action.

Shouting, "We must protect a woman's right to choose by keeping abortion legal!" is like saying, "We must protect a man's right to choose by letting him use a flamethrower to incinerate a house!" The capacity to act doesn't always justify action. Because we have a flamethrower, we might have the capacity to incinerate a house, but it doesn't logically proceed that we *should* do so, for it might be someone else's home.

To divert attention away from the futility of their pro-choice argument, mainstream abortion organizations pivot from exclusively using the term "pro-choice," and deploy other terms like, "pro-reproductive rights." It's nothing more than subterfuge. The argument for abortion on the grounds that it upholds "pro-reproductive rights," is just the same old "pro-choice" argument seasoned with a different spice. All activists mean when they say, "pro-reproductive rights" is the ability to exercise those rights, and choose to abort their children.

While certainly not the only example, abortion is a demonstration of the belief society calls *progressivism.* People champion abortion because it's the progressive thing to do, evolving our society away from ancient patriarchy, and instead, thrusting it into the future. Put simply, progressivism is the state of **doing what's right in one's own eyes**, and it's the entire focus of this book.

Political leaders and activists force our society to pursue progressivism purely because it's the progressive thing to do. Of course, the cutting problem with progressivism is that it isn't progressive. The very ideal of progress doesn't itself progress, and worshipping it causes self-destruction.

Aristotle knew this, even in antiquity. He understood it's impossible to worship change, because it means worshipping an ideal that's constant and unchanging. Likewise, worshipping progress means worshipping a stagnant and fixed standard. While everything around the progressive moves through time and space, his worship of progress means he commits its unforgivable sin, as he never progresses to worshipping something else.

I've sometimes heard well-meaning, conservative commentators call progressivism "regressive," but it can't really be called that, either. We can't label progressivism "progressive" or "regressive," because progressivism means the destruction of objective standards. "Right and wrong, good and evil, forward and backward," all become terms without meaning. In a progressive world, there's nothing to measure those words against, so there's nothing to establish moral direction. Today, a progressive believes in social reform *t, u, v.* Tomorrow, as long as it's the progressive thing to do, he'll believe in social reform *x, y, z.*

To better understand this problem, think about a progressive marathon. In such an event it's not like participants are running backward during the race, it's that they don't know which way to run. No one can definitively say whether a man is farther away, or closer to, the finish line because the finish line must always be in flux, never fixed in a particular place.

Normally, a fluctuating finish line is a problem, but not in a progressive race. The object of a progressive marathon isn't to cross the finish line first and win. Rather, the object is to run forever. Even if progressive runners catch a glimpse of the finish line, and run towards it as fast as they can, they'll never cross it. At the moment they're about to do so, they crash with a deafening halt, not into other runners, but into a paradox.

If marathon runners cross the finish line, they cease to progress towards the line, and the dogma of their progressivism dies. Using progressivism to achieve anything guarantees its suicide. A finish line turns into a blasphemous thing, because once runners cross the line, there's no more race left to run, and no more "progress" left to pursue.

For progressives, the very existence of a finish line, moving around the map or not, is an affront, because it implies completion. If they ever achieve anything at all, their progress stops, and they're forced to either cannibalize their beliefs and destroy their ideological foundations, or embark on an insane journey of "progressing" forever and ever. Thus, in an act of desperation, progressive marathon runners don't deny that they're running toward the finish line; they don't even deny the fantastic statement that the finish line is running toward them. Instead, they deny the *existence* of the finish line.

Because a fixed objective is the mortal enemy of progressivism, progressives, like most modern politicians, prefer to pursue abstract ideals. Take climate change, for example. It's no wonder our leaders are so infatuated with it. The climate, like progressivism, perpetually changes.

The weather's always fluctuating. The fact that our climate's in a constant state of change is a changeless fact. Politicians latch on to the goal of "stopping climate change," knowing full well the climate's going to change, forever. Doing so lets them activate whatever policies and powers they wish, for as long as they wish, in the name of achieving something that's never going to be achieved.

In this, the progressive ideal of progress isn't actually progress. To see this clearly, compare the climate change fiasco to a real example of progress, like a man building a new skyscraper in his city. We can tell whether he's progressing toward his goal or not, because we can see the skyscraper being built. His objective is fixed and measurable. First, he starts by clearing land, then he pours cement, hires ironworkers, carpenters, and electricians, and begins building higher and higher. In no time at all, a new skyscraper, it's roof freshly completed, dominates the horizon of downtown, proving the investor has completed his project. His objective's been achieved. It's a real type of progress, and progressives hate it.

The difference between building a skyscraper and combating climate change is that building a skyscraper produces tangible, verifiable, results. If an investor tells us he needs carpenters, we can understand why when we watch the concrete for the skyscraper being poured. But when eco-radicals tell us to turn off our furnaces, they fail to provide any evidence showing that their strategy to save the Earth (whatever that means) is working.

No one knows what it'll take to achieve government's climate objectives, because no one knows what the objectives are. One day activists say it's too hot, the next day they say it's too cold, and even if the day after is just right, they say perfection is indicative of artificial human meddling with the climate they worship.

When we ask our governments exactly what their climate objectives are, their answers are explicitly vague for a reason. If they provide measurable numbers and goals, our society might one day achieve them, and government's excuse of imposing harsh regulations in the name of "saving the Earth" would no longer be acceptable.

We have no doubt they yearn to prolong this everlasting war as long as they can. Even if we foolishly freed ourselves from oil and gas, it still wouldn't be enough for our leaders. They'd make us trek even further into the jungle of eco-progressivism, until we were hailed villains for living under jack pines, and industrial tycoons for stripping the bark off a birch.

These examples of progressivism are all too common in modern political spheres. Some time ago, in the Canadian

Federal Election, the slogan of the victorious Mr. Justin Trudeau and his Liberal Party was, "Forward. For everyone."

What does Mr. Trudeau and his political strategists mean by "Forward?" Forward toward what? They don't have an immovable standard of right and wrong. How can they claim to move in any direction?

Not only so but like so many other politicians around the world, Trudeau promises to "Build Back Better." Again, what does he mean by "Better?" Prime Minister Trudeau is among the most famous progressives in the world. To him, objective law is what light is to a vampire, and what sin is to a saint. How can he claim to move the country, "Forward. For everyone," while refusing to consult a moral map? How can he say, in this matrix of morality, whether Canada's moving forward or backward? Mr. Trudeau can't claim to move the country in any direction, because he doesn't have a moral compass telling him where to go.

Instead, our Prime Minister's like a spaceman who's lost in the cosmos without a frame of reference. The only difference is that while the spaceman's looking into a dark physical void, Mr. Trudeau's looking into a moral one. As the spaceman, without a frame of physical reference, has no idea what up, down, backward, and forward means, Mr. Trudeau, without a moral reference, has no idea what good, bad, right, wrong, just, and unjust mean. The best he can do (or the worst he can do, depending on how one looks at it), is make up his own definitions and impose them upon us.

How then can the Canadian Prime Minster possibly claim to "Build Back Better?" His ideology doesn't allow him to hit "better" targets, only different ones. For progressives, the term "better" can't even exist, because it implies an objective standard beyond themselves, which is precisely the thing they're rebelling against. Besides, when one looks at what our governments are trying to impose, it's clear they're not "Building Back Better." They're not even building. Instead, they're trying to destroy.

Like anything unrighteous and evil, the best way to resist progressivism is to resist it before it exists. Regrettably, it's too late for that, so we have to deploy our second-best strategy: a valiant offence. Perhaps it's best to do so by asking if the progressive actually cares about proper progress. Like Mr. Trudeau, most progressives excel in demolishing a society, rather than constructing one.

"Well yes," they might reply, "but we have to tear down old buildings to put new ones up. We have to crush the old morality to replace it with the new."

The problem with the analogy is that progressives aren't just tearing down buildings; they're demolishing the foundations upon which society stands. The rational thing to do is accept the intrinsic beauty, legitimacy, and *necessity* of the old morality, while also building upon it to make it better. For example, while it's good that a man avoids committing adultery with his neighbour, it's not good enough. He must also not lust after her in his heart. Or, while it's good that a child doesn't hit his classmates, he must be actively kind to them, as well. That's what real moral progress looks like. It's what the Scriptures teach in Matthew 5:21-22 when it says, "*You have heard that it was said to those of old, 'You shall not murder; and whoever murders will be liable to judgment.' But I say to you that everyone who is angry with his brother will be liable to judgment; whoever insults his brother will be liable to the council; and whoever says, 'You fool!' will be liable to the hell of fire.'*"

In *Abolition of Man,* C.S. Lewis compares such moral advance to a man who wants fresh vegetables. "You like to buy your vegetables moderately fresh," Lewis says, "why not grow your own and have them perfectly fresh?" It's like saying, "You like a comfortable home. Why not install air conditioning, and a sunroom, to make it even more comfortable than it is right now?"[2]

But progressives advocate for no such thing. Instead, they say something along the lines of, "You like your vegetables moderately fresh, so throw them out and start playing with bricks." Or, "You like a comfortable home, why not push your car into the ocean?" Their advice isn't just wrong, it's totally insane.

There's a reason no one's ever heard of a post-modern, progressive, architect. They don't exist. Any that might've existed flunked out of school. But suppose there were progressive architects. What would their buildings look like? Their buildings wouldn't look like anything, because there wouldn't be any buildings to look at. All of their progressive architecture, constructed with progressive ideals in mind, would be nothing more than heaps of rubble. How could they be anything else?

Architecture requires laws of construction, called "blueprints." A truly progressive architect couldn't stomach such laws, because it imposes a set of intolerable restrictions upon his artistic vision. But we need those rules. Without them, we might set our studs 48 inches apart on centre, or pour ½ inch of concrete in the basement, and act like everything's fine as the house comes crumbling down.

I, for one, am very glad an architect who understands the importance of foundations and blueprints built my home; I hope progressive couples living in their homes feel the same.

---

[2] C.S Lewis, *The Abolition of Man* (New York: HarperCollins, 2001), 46.

But while man is the builder of homes, God is the builder of everything, and, like blueprints telling us that studs 48 inches apart are dangerous, the blueprints for life tell us that progressivism is wrong.

To summarize this chapter, we've reached a fulcrum in our society where we're progressing because we have to. We never stop. We progress purely for the purpose of progressing. The journey toward the end has become the end, but with progressivism, there is no end.

Rational men stop driving when they reach the campsite. Progressives aren't driving to any particular destination. Hikers finish their climbs and enjoy the views at the mountaintop. Progressive hikers hate the mountain peaks, because it means their hike's completed. For progressives, the journey is their destination. The hike is their summit.

However, there's such a thing as driving too far; there's such a thing as hiking too high. If you never stop driving, you discover you've driven nowhere. It doesn't mean you've arrive at some secret oasis; it means that you're lost. Or, if you never stop hiking, you fall over the other side of the mountain. It doesn't mean you discover some new cave for spelunking; it means you've fallen to your death.

The progressive's hunger for the future means he commits the primal sins of the past. His infatuation for the new means he strives to be like the old. We're told we live in a modern epoch, but as it turns out, we've turned our society into a modern Jericho.

We're not a modern society; we're a biblical one. We're like Israel when the book of Judges concludes, precisely because we have no judge. Progressives demand everything becomes progressive, except the society's belief in progressivism. We're forced to tolerate everything, even though progressivism's intolerant of anything other than itself. We've sacrificed all, even our children, to the god of progressivism. There's only one thing left to offer on the altar: *Ourselves.*

We used to chop down landscapes to save men, but now we chop down men to save landscapes. Israel persecuted the prophets, but we persecute the pastors. Carthage sacrificed children to the fires of Baal, but we rip them apart, limb by limb, while they're weeping in the womb. Adam and Eve were excommunicated from the Garden of God, but a Saviour's opened it for us again. However, because that would mean ceasing our progress, even though we're progressing toward Hell, we refuse to return.

CHAPTER 2

The Kingdom of Education

Modern educators love to virtue signal, offer territory acknowledgements, and declare our schools sit on stolen land. Strangely, it seems none of the educators are serious or convicted enough to give the land back.

Students attend arithmetic and learn that one doesn't equal two. Later, their grammar teacher introduces himself by saying, "My name is Jones, and I use 'they/them' pronouns," as though an individual can be two or more. Of course, if Jones were serious about his identity and grammar, he would correct his diction and say, "*we* go by them/them pronouns," instead of, "*I* go by they/them pronouns."

We remember going to English class, hoping to learn how to communicate like civilized English men. Instead, we got lessons on why everyone should hate Englishmen. Once upon a time, all of us were proud to stand for the anthem. Today, ideologues teach their students why they should be ashamed when the anthem's played. In science, high school students learn all about objective human biology, and why it's so important to study and understand. In health, these same students learn all about why human biology isn't objective or important at all.

Though we don't have time to talk about them, there are many more examples of these ideological contradictions our children are learning in school. Regardless, it's clear that education's coming to a point where left is right, up is down, freedom is slavery, and truth is a lie. We often hear that humans are logical creatures, but a one-minute examination of many voters has us thinking we're the farthest thing from logical. Nevertheless, because we're made in the image of Almighty God, we've been endowed with the inherent capacity for rationality and reason; currently, many public schools are trying to lock all of that away.

It's no wonder public [government] schools work their hardest to make students irrational and unreasonable. Public schools are usually progressive schools, and progressives have to brainwash students with logical contradictions because progressivism is logically contradictory. The only way to believe in progressivism is to believe in anything, even insane absurdities, because progressivism *is* an insane absurdity.

Orwell describes it best in his book *1984*. To make people in dystopian Oceana believe in perpetual war, Big Brother and the party hammer into their minds the idea that, "War is peace." Constant fighting comes to mean the absence of fighting. Citizens learn they can't live in a world without war, because that would mean war.

To take another example, Big Brother and the party control every aspect of the citizen's life. Normally, people call that "slavery," but Big Brother beats them to the punch, and says, "Freedom is slavery." Doing so lets Big Brother insinuate that slavery is freedom." Thus, people in Oceana can't live without being told what to do, because then they'd be slaves to their own freedom.

Finally, in Orwell's Oceana, every piece of history is altered or destroyed. We know that neglecting the knowledge of the past weakens our knowledge of the present and future, but in Oceana, "Ignorance is strength." Knowledge is power, but in *1984,* knowledge is frailty. The citizens under Big Brother think they're strong, because they no longer know what strength means.

Orwell's previous three examples of semantic absurdity are logically ridiculous, and that's the point. If man believes in one contradiction, why not two? The moment he tolerates one statement of rational ridiculousness is the moment he tolerates them all. The same is true with progressivism. If we needed to create three slogans for their cause, we might say, "Love is hate, singular is plural, and man is woman."

We already live in a world where 1+0=2, or 2+2=5, because individuals have pronouns "they/them." We live in a nation that's pro-choice, but believes in stealing everyone's choice if they don't agree with the narrative. We're forced to progress in every area of life, except in our worship of progress. Nothing makes sense, so progressives say everything is sensical.

The reason our students are targeted with this insanity is because they're still building their foundations of value, morality, and reality. As adults, we have those foundations in place. While it is not impossible for grown-ups to adopt a radically different set of beliefs than their own, it's unusual to hear of such change. Transformative beliefs rarely penetrate to the heart of an old man's soul.

Children, however, are different. They're like sponges, soaking up every piece of information we provide, using it all to construct their vision about the world. Radical educators know this, and seize the opportunity to create new soldiers of progressivism by teaching our youth contemptible values in class.

At the end of all their brainwashing, children are so exhausted and confused about reality they regrettably capitulate and say, "I guess the world can be whatever I want. I can do whatever I feel is right in my own eyes. After all, if my teachers can contradict logic and believe in anything, why can't I?"

In this, while the old way to achieve good grades in class was to think, the new way to achieve good grades in class is to stop thinking and let the educator think for you. In *The Abolition of Man,* C.S. Lewis says, "The task of the modern educator is not to cut down jungles, but to irrigate deserts."[3] He knows that young students are often intellectually under stimulated and starved for mental exercise. In an age where they get everything at the click of a button, their imaginations dry up like abandoned wells. The perceived drudgery of real life compared to the virtual one makes the world look grey and dull.

Thus, part of the teacher's critical mission is reviving the student's vitality for exploration while encouraging intellectual rejuvenation. Their job means exposing the student to the real world, and watering his desire to think for himself. However, our bureaucrats conclude precisely the opposite. While Lewis says, "The task of the modern educator is not to cut down jungles, but to irrigate deserts," the current bureaucrat says,

[3] Lewis, *The Abolition of Man*, 13-14.

"The task of the modern educator is not to irrigate deserts, but to cut down jungles."

While our worry is that students are intellectually paralyzed, progressives argue that students are intellectually overwhelmed. They say the pressing crisis relates to what children are being taught online, on TV, and dare we speak, in the *home.* They act like it's not only overwhelming, but dangerous. After all, who knows if what our children are learning behind closed doors is tolerant or loving? What if their parents are dreadfully capitalist, conservative, Bible-believing Christians wanting to teach their children proper values? We even know that educators have the ability to hide a child's change in pronouns from his or her parents. They do so on the grounds that it's safer for the child, acting as if youth don't need to be exposed to their homes, but protected from them.

Of course, children are rewarded by their schools when they perfectly adhere to this new-age education, so our society often confuses obedience with intelligence. Our "thinkers" have been trained from their youth to blindly follow their superiors, whether activists disguised as teachers, or powerful politicians decorated as meek old men. That's why so many modern "intellectuals" (who often aren't very intellectual at all) capitulate to unintellectual dogmas. Obeying authority without question is all they've ever known.

For progressive educators, eager students are easiest to brainwash and convert to this modern god of godlessness. Their hunger to succeed and be acknowledged for their efforts means they do just about anything, internalizing every lesson and repeating every lecture verbatim, to impress educators administering their grades. These students don't need to be lured, tricked, or coerced into accepting wrong ideals and beliefs; they come to the altar of ideological slaughter willingly, perfectly content to be falsely indoctrinated in exchange for a smiley face at the top of their final exam.

People see a 98% on the top of an essay, and conclude it means the student's an excellent writer. Perhaps that's true, but perhaps it means the student simply wrote a trailblazing treatise on how evil capitalism is. Intelligent classmates used to be those who thought outside the box, but now, they're those who never so much as look outside the box, let alone leave it. As brain-dead students are hailed academics, and cautious students are labelled backwater conservatives, we shudder with the realization that the old intellectuals were those who thought, but the new intellectuals are those who do not think.

Progressive schools' willingness to sacrifice truth for obedience extends beyond letter grades. To see what I mean, think about a young man in class named Johnathan. The truth is that Johnathan's a biological male, but he chooses to act and dress like a woman. His educators in class sacrifice the truth, and exalt Johnathan repeatedly for his courageous choice. They shower him with putrid praise for rejecting what's real, acting as if living in a lie is somehow superior to submitting to reality. Classmates, teachers, superintendents, and school boards, tell Johnathan he can be whatever, or whoever, he wants to be. If he wants to be a female, he can be a female. If he wants to be a woman, then a woman he shall become.

In a modern ritual, educators chant and cheer Johnathan's rebellion against the Almighty, and if any students refuse to take part in this evil manipulation, they're labelled oppressive, hateful, intolerant, transphobic, and homophobic. Granted, the same accusers who call people "transphobic" or "homophobic" for refusing to accept that a man can be a woman, would call people "hydrophobic" for refusing to accept that a car can drive in the ocean. Let them mock rationality all they want; reality doesn't care. If such activists dare put their beliefs to the test and plunge their vehicles into the Atlantic, they'll sink to the bottom of the sea, along with their ideals.

Likewise, the male Johnathan can mock reality and pretend to be a woman if he chooses. He changes his name to "Joanne." His educators and classmates reinforce his lie, and tell him he's as female as Princess Diana, or Aphrodite as long as he lives, but he doesn't have XX chromosomes, and eventually, Johnathan grows a beard, gains muscle mass, lowers his voice, and woefully discovers he's unable to bear children.

Progressive schools don't care. The Lord Almighty says, "I made this young man to be a man, and a man he's going to be." Public educators say, "This a young man, if he wants to be a man, can dress however he wants, act however he wants, and believe he's whoever he wants! If he wants to be a woman, then we're going to treat him like a woman. If he wants to rebel against creation, then we're going to march alongside him in his crusade."

The rebellion against creation comes in the fact that in the Garden of Eden, God tells christened mankind that there are two genders. The Scripture says, "Male and female He created them" (Genesis 5:2). It doesn't say man can choose to be woman or woman can choose to be man, nor does it say Adam and Eve can transition to either gender whenever they choose. God doesn't give them a choice in the matter, because gender is sacred.

However, instead of telling Johnathan, "God made you to be male," his teachers tell him, "You can be whatever, and whoever, you want to be! You don't need to listen to God, precisely because you're the god of your own world. Refuse to accept your current gender? Do what's right in your own eyes, get an irreversible reassignment surgery, and transition to something alien! Destroy Almighty's creation, and turn yourself into a foreigner against His contemptible plan. We'll affirm all of your choices, even if it leads you down a path of life where all your future choices are taken away."

Part of the reason our educators are so cowardly, refusing to correct their students when they reject reality, is because they follow the famous dogma of Miss Margaret Mead. She says, "The children must be taught how to think, not what to think."[4] and her views infect our educational institutions.

She couldn't be more wrong, nor can her beliefs be more damaging to society. Someone ought to have asked her, "You say, 'Children must be taught how to think, not what to think,' but isn't that telling us what to think and not how to think? Aristotle stands defiantly against the feminist, and so does Plato. The Proverbs oppose her beliefs, and the Scriptures vehemently deny the legitimacy of her creed. All of them are clear in their condemnation of Mead, and teach that children must not only be taught *what* to think before they're taught *how* to think, but if they're not taught *what* to think, they'll never *be* able to think!

Think about it. When a man refuses to act rationally, we tell him, "You're not thinking straight!" In order for us to say so, we have to have some idea what "thinking straight" means. But if children (and people) must be taught how to think, not what to think, no one's conclusion on anything can ever be wrong. As long as men are thinking, they are "thinking straight."

[4] Margaret Mead, *Coming of Age In Samoa* https://archive.org/stream/in.ernet.dli.2015.189627/2015.189627.Coming-Of-Age-In-Samoa-Margaret-Mead_djvu.txt. Date accessed Jan 2, 2024.

In reality, men aren't thinking straight when their conclusions are perverted. We know what they're supposed to think about the colour of sun, and if they argue it's blue, their thinking's wrong. Education's the same. It's true that we ought to teach our children how to perform proper arithmetic, and use proper grammar, but we also have to teach them what the correct conclusions are. If a student performs mathematical operations and arrives at the wrong answer, he's done something incorrect, and it needs to be fixed.

Likewise, it's only after children are taught what to think about morality and learn to ground themselves in foundations of self-evident principles, that they can think like mature adults. If our children are not taught what to think before they're taught to think, when it comes time to think about something serious, their thinking will be useless—even deadly.

For example, a physics teacher instructs his students about acceleration, speed, gravity, and air resistance. The students, learning *how* to think about physics, apply their lessons, and calculate the speed and trajectory of a bullet fired from a gun.

That's all fine and well, but unless the students also learn what to think about morality, they won't be able to apply their mathematical conclusions in the real world. Sure, they might be able to say, "Based on our calculations, the bullet travels at 830 feet per second," but that doesn't tell them whether they should shoot the innocent man, or not. Other scientists might confidently conclude, "The virus will travel this far and this fast," but that doesn't tell them whether they should lock down the nation or keep it free.

Now, see what happens if we teach people what to think before they're taught how to think. Once again, the young scientists might discover that the bullet travels 830 feet/second. However, this time, they finish their thought with, "but we must never shoot the innocent man." Virologists might calculate the speed and severity of a virus, knowing the mental, economic, and spiritual, health of a nation must also be accounted for.

"Well, hold on just a moment," interjects Jones, the modern educator. "Why should *you* be allowed to impose *your* values in the classroom? Why should our schools impose a Judeo-Christian worldview, instead of a Muslim, progressive, or Inuit one? As educators, we forfeit the right to transmit personal values to students through our teaching, so we approach our lessons from a neutral point of view. If a child wants to be transgender, we have no right to discourage that process, because we'd be imposing personal, negative bias. If a child wants to believe that 2+2=5, we have no right to tell him he's wrong. Everyone has their own truth. Everyone has their own values. All we're called to do is teach the lessons handed down to us from curriculum authors above."

We'll answer Jones' question later, but not before charging him with being the perfect hypocrite. His judgement to *not* impose a worldview upon students is itself a worldview. The statements, "we shouldn't teach morals," and, "We should teach morals," both appeal to some form of morality. Thus, not only do educators impress their morality upon the students they teach, its impossible for them to *not* do so.

I'm hearing more and more often this strange conviction, even amongst conservatives, that education must be divorced from morality. You might as well try to divorce the oxygen atom from a water molecule. Progressives want to divorce education from morality because they think conservatives indoctrinate children at home; conservatives want to divorce education from morality because they believe progressives indoctrinate children in class. Both sides of the spectrum argue teachers have no right or reason to transmit their morality upon students. The problem with both views is that the plain act of education *is* the transmission of morals and values. Not only do teachers impress their values on children, but the idea that anyone can educate without doing so is a preposterous lie.

Trying to separate education from morals is like saying, "I'd like a ribeye steak, as long as you don't slaughter any cows," or, "I'd like to quench my thirst, without drinking any liquid." The act of education, and the act of transmitting morals, are one in the same. If you do not teach morality and values, you do not teach.

For example, suppose teacher Jones assigns a paper in history class. On its due date, 24 out of 29 classmates submit their assignments, but five of them miss the deadline. Instead of failing those students who aren't diligent enough to hand in their essays on time, the teacher says, "No worries, I'll extend the deadline another day or two. I won't mark the papers for a little while anyway."

Jones' decision to tolerate disobedience and failure incurs reverberating consequences for his class. Whether he knows it or not, he's teaching a deafening lesson about work ethic and fairness. By agreeing to extend the deadline of the paper for those students who failed to hand in their work on time, Jones shows the entire class he doesn't reward diligence or hard work, so they shouldn't strive for it. He's promoting a progressive worldview where everyone enjoys equality of outcome instead of equality of opportunity. Although he might not explicitly teach this dogma, he still insinuates the lazy, entitled sentiment into every student's mind. If deadlines don't matter, what's the point of meeting them? If Jones is just going to extend duc dates anyway, why work to meet his demands?

Some 10 or 20 years into the future, their teacher forgotten and his lectures catalogued deep into the recesses of their subconscious, the grown-up students throw tantrums when society doesn't meet their every demand. Why work hard? Why achieve excellence? The fact that their coworkers receive $5000 more per year more than they do is intolerable, even though their coworkers do more work, because it's precisely the opposite of what Jones taught them in school.

By now, the failure of Miss Margaret Mead's entire belief is obvious. Mead and her disciples in modern education demand we teach children *how* to think and not *what* to think. As a matter of fact, even if one only teaches a child *how* to think, he ends up teaching him *what* to think.

Mead's belief contradicts itself. If children are not taught what to think, they are not taught, for the act of teaching is instructing children what to think. Fail to teach students the importance about deadlines, and they'll formulate false views about deadlines. Refuse to teach them about the dangers of lying, and they'll come to accept that lying's fine. Tolerate all their choices, and they'll become the least tolerant tyrants on the planet.

To visualize this problem, here's a lesson for educators from an actual early-learning curriculum. I've edited the names and scenario for the purposes of this book, but the principle of the story's exactly the same.

Think about an early-learning educator named "Sarah" teaching a student named "Cash." In the morning, Cash plays with a toy truck until, when it's time for lunch, Sarah tells the class to clean up their items. Cash begins to disobey. He refuses to part with his truck. He doesn't want to put his toy away, and when he's told to do so, he acts like he can't hear.

The proper recourse for such behaviour is justified discipline, teaching Cash what to think about disobedience in the face of legitimate authority. He needs to learn that disobeying a just command is inexcusable and wrong. He doesn't need to be taught *how* to think about his disobedience, he needs to be taught *what* to think about it (i.e. that it's unacceptable).

But the curriculum doesn't recommend Sarah do that.

Instead, the curriculum has Sarah make Cash feel as comfortable as possible. According to the authors, Cash needs to know his feelings are heard, that his teacher cares for him, and that she takes his emotional state seriously. Sarah's supposed to act with sensitivity and respect, speaking to Cash with gentle, cooing, words, while also negotiating a compromise. That is, Cash can keep the toy if he keeps it in his cubby, and not in the toy container where it belongs. Having won the battle, he agrees, and enjoys lunchtime with his friends.

Although they might not understand it yet, and although they might not intend for it to happen, the curriculum authors, and Sarah, are turning Cash into a monster. From his brief encounter with Sarah (an encounter that will no doubt be repeated), Cash comes to learn his emotions and feelings are equivalent to reason and moral goodness. Like any dedicated progressive, He begins to believe his emotions *are* reason and moral goodness.

Cash quickly comes to accept, and accepts for the rest of his life, that his emotions and personal happiness are the standard of right and wrong that others must follow and obey. Every order he receives is to be tested against the comfort of his body and soul. Commands which invoke anxiety or discomfort shall be disregarded, and subsequently disobeyed.

For Cash, objective rules and regulations no longer exist. The only rules that exist are subjective ones he deems are agreeable. He's no longer ruled by a set of rules; he becomes the set of rules. He's no longer commanded by a superior; he *is* the superior, and his feelings of newfound supremacy don't die with a diploma. Thanks to his education, his happiness is his compass. He follows his fickle feelings, and lets them guide his life. Maybe that's why our society is so plagued with tragedies like divorce.

Divorce is so tragic and typical of our progressive society. Why shouldn't it be? Marriage is a rock and pillar of human civilization, but progressivism tears every foundation down, including our sacred relationships that build society up. People possess stronger loyalties for their favourite hockey teams than they do for their spouses. They care more for a sport's team that's given them nothing—not even a playoff victory in the last 20 years—than they do for their husbands or wives who've given them everything they have, including themselves.

At one moment, two separate souls pledge transcendental allegiance and fidelity to one another, promising at the altar, "Till death do us part." But a little while later, that same couple says to each other, "You're going to be the death of me if we do not part!" More and more spouses are changing their vows from, "Because I love you, I'm doing what you will," to the progressive, "Because I love myself, I'm doing what I want."

Progressives argue that even though marriage might be a rock and pillar of society, it's a rock that's getting in their way. They call it an obtrusive, obstructive, patriarchal rock, symbolizing female oppression, and denying people a path in life they think they'd rather follow.

Not only are the progressives wrong, but even if they realize that marriage is a rock, they fail to realize (or fail to care) that it's not some random rock. Rather, it's a carefully constructed cornerstone, upon which the whole apparatus of civilization rests.

Marriage is a foundation of civilized society and human nature, and even though ideologues believe it's an archaic institution that no longer applies in our feminist epoch, if they rebelliously remove the rock in the name of "progress," the entire structure of society collapses and crushes them from above. In the wake of its rubble, our nations are left exposed, and the hideous monsters of promiscuity, hedonism, and licentiousness are activated, eager to devour everyone whole.

Another reason we have a surplus of divorce, just like how we have a surplus of abortion, transgenderism, and promiscuity, is because progressives in all areas of society make divorce sound so easy and painless. However, like just about everything else the progressive believes and preaches, that's a lie. There's nothing easy or painless about divorce. Men and women can try and deny the severity of breaking a couple apart and say divorce is what happens when a man and wife "split up." But divorce isn't splitting up; divorce is shattering into a million pieces, and that's indescribably more painful.

You can't cut a married couple in two anymore than you can slice a perfect plane of glass in half by dropping it on a concrete floor, so why do people still furiously believe that divorce is what happens when separate people go their separate ways? Besides, it's not like the only parties harmed in a divorce are the husband and wife. There are other innocents, torn shreds by the shrapnel of court appearances and proceedings, caught in the crossfire of marital battles that end in disaster.

As a child of preachers and Bible Camp directors, growing up, I spent almost all of my summers working at Bible camp. During those years, I met tens of thousands of campers and families from a diverse catalogue of culture, age, spirituality, and wealth. Although each camper was entirely unique, the one constant among all of them, apart from the haunting silence that washed over them during every salvation message we ever gave, was that the rowdiest, angriest, most poorly-behaved children were from divorced families.

As counsellors, we never needed more than an hour to divine a sketch of the campers' lives at home. Although we never would, we never needed to ask camper, "Are your parents married or divorced?" The child's actions, demeanor, and temperament answered for us. I'm not saying an unalterable law exists that states, "Children from divorced families are more difficult to deal with than their nuclear-family counterparts." Rather, I'm saying every worker at camp noticed an unmistakable trend in that, 99 times out of 100, if a camper was a struggle to counsel, he lived in a broken home.

I know that broken homes and behaviour are correlated, because as campers from divorced homes opened up to their counsellors, they told us it was so. They told us how excruciating it was to be trapped in the middle of their parents' divorce, and they told us how horrible it was to go before a judge and choose which parent they loved most. Listening to these stories meant every counsellor quickly learned that when a marriage is broken, children break as well. More often than not, a camper's obnoxious and messy behaviour was a desperate cry for attention, perhaps because they received so little meaningful attention anywhere else.

We knew better than to counter a camper's outburst with frustration or anger; he heard enough of that at home. Instead, the way to respond was with compassion, for the more abrasive a child was on the outside, the more delicate his fragile little soul tended to be. We often think a damaged soul is a broken soul, searing hot with rage, but it's not. A damaged soul is an impenetrable fortress, closed off to the rest of the world in defiance and frightened defense, colder than the loneliest stone.

It's now clear that adults are often progressive because they're taught progressivism in their youth. We can conclude that much of modern education is to blame for our society's belief in progressivism, but who "educated" the modern educators? Certain teachers teach their students to do what's right in their own eyes, but who taught the teachers to teach that? And who taught their teachers' teachers?

Unless we are able to stop at some point and say, "This is where progressivism started; this is where the dogma originated," we spiral into an illogical infinite regress of questions without answers. After all, there are numerous examples of society doing what's right in its own eyes long before government-run education was even considered, so where did progressivism start?

Who was the first one who rebelled against reality, and what were their motives for doing so? Who was the first one that said, "Even though a rebellion against reality causes personal, serious, suffering, and even though everyone else will suffer because of it, it's better than living in reality?"

To find out, I searched through the history books and travelled back further and further in time. Finally, I arrived at a mystical oasis, shrouded in perfection and Heavenly mist in the Garden of Eden.

I found a simple story that depicted two people turning into progressives, doing what was right in their own eyes, and eating the fruit from the Tree of the Knowledge of Good and Evil. However, as I was reading, I was struck with a revelation. Adam and Eve weren't the first progressives, because someone, or *something,* tempted them to sin. In an instant, I realized the human race learned progressivism from something *that hated humanity.* Perhaps that explains why progressivism is so antihuman.

Intrigued, I travelled back even further in time by travelling further ahead in the Bible (Revelation 12). Finally, I arrived at the answer to our question, "Where did progressivism start?"

The architect of progressivism is the author of arrogance and pride. The last place one would think to find progressivism is the first place that it started. In the Throne Room of Truth Himself, progressivism was born from angel of light whom God created named Lucifer. He's the first creature ever to say, "I will do what's right in my own eyes," before tempting us to do exactly the same.

We'd be wise to heed a warning. Although Lucifer tried to glorify himself greater than YAHWEH, and although his blasphemous proclamation of supremacy reverberated throughout Heaven, God's already rendered His judgement, and the fallen angel's eternity is sealed in the hottest fires of Hell.

CHAPTER 3

The Kingdom of Socialism

I've never understood why socialists call themselves socialists. What's the point in doing so when there's nothing social about their ideology? Socialism's the supreme breed of selfishness, infecting people with a more severe allergy to charity than anything comparable in capitalist nations.

The most socialist politicians in public tend to be the least socialist people in private. They say they're generous, wanting to share everything with everyone, but they're generous with all the wrong things. Instead of being generous with their money, they're generous with *our* money. Instead of being generous with freedom, they're generous with tyranny. They're generous in their control, oppression, and coercion, while greedily hoarding any kindness, benevolence, mercy, or compassion, they might have left in their bodies.

Thus, people suffering under a socialist regime can't share anything with anyone, because there aren't any spare goods or services to share. There aren't even enough goods and services for people to meet their own needs, let alone the needs of their neighbours.

No one shares meals, because there isn't enough food for each person to begin with. No one shares clothes, because everyone's already wearing worn-out, dirty rags. Families fight for scraps of mouldy bread. If it's legal for them to do so, people scrounge around garbage bins for anything they can use. There are no charities in socialist worlds because no one has enough money to be charitable. If a cashier at the socialist supermarket asks his customer, "Can you spare a dollar to feed the poor?" the shopper merely replies, "I am the poor."

As socialism spreads like a virus throughout a nation, people are scolded and told they care too deeply for their material possessions. "Capitalism," it's said, "cultivates a hideous greed in men for material items. We have to free ourselves of such slavery, and turn our nation into a socialist paradise where private ownership no longer exists."

Ironically, man's desire for his material possessions doesn't die in socialist nations. He isn't freed from his love of physical goods when his government declares no one owns anything. Instead, his love for what he has burns more fiercely than it ever did before.

Clueless, progressive, narcissistic, ideologues, like 21-year-old student activists in university arrogantly assert that only the rich care about material possession and private property. If the ideologues opened their eyes and spent even a day in the real world, they'd realize how wrong they are. It's true that the rich care about their property. That's what makes them rich. But the poor care about property, too, and they often care about it with a more fervent desperation in their eyes. If a rich man loses something, like a coat, he shrugs his shoulders, goes to the store, and buys another. But if a poor man loses a coat, he loses almost everything he has, so he moves Heaven and Earth to try and get it back. The more socialist a nation becomes, the poorer men become; the poorer they become, the more they love the few material possessions they secretly own.

In capitalist nations, families throw out rotten blankets when they're tattered and torn. After all, they can simply walk to the store and purchase new blankets whenever they please. The same isn't true in socialist nations. There, no one throws out blankets, no matter how putrid and spoiled the blankets are, because no one knows if a new shipment of blankets will ever arrive. Socialist victims cling to every material possession they have—thin slippers, broken dishes, disintegrating shoes—because they are the only possessions they're able to call theirs.

In this, Mr. Chesterton's correct when he says, "Socialists assume that private property was never anything but a sort of crude capitalistic luxury; and they are very much startled when they collide with the peasant and find the strongest sense of property is not found in the world of luxury, but in the world of poverty."[5] However, my chief concern isn't that socialists are startled when they discover the overwhelming sense of property among the poor; it's that the socialists are no longer startled, and no longer care.

They no longer care because, as socialists, their purpose *isn't* to create utopia. The economic condition of the people doesn't matter, as long as the party, under the cover of economic revolution, achieves terrible political, moral, and *progressive* reform in the nation.

---

[5] G.K. Chesterton, (@GKCdaily), Twitter, August 20, 2019, https://twitter.com/GKCdaily/status/1163681412479901696.

A ruthless socialism imposed means people might be afflicted with horrendous suffering, but progressives say their anguish is of no consequence. The wails of socialism are treated like nothing more than the screams of patients in a hospital. Socialist leaders fashion themselves surgeons, trying to heal an economy like doctors working to fix a man's broken bone. It might be painful for the patient; it might even be excruciating, but all of his suffering is acceptable in the grand design of health and security.

In pursuit of a socialist world, perhaps a "few" citizens lose their life savings, or adopt strict diets because groceries are unacceptably scarce. But all of those sacrifices are trivial compared to the triumphs of collective ownership. Rationing what little power they have, or living off stale, mouldy, bread, are mere unavoidable inconveniences in the grand scheme of gaining freedom from capitalist oppression. One has to break some eggs to make an omelet, innocent men have to die to win the war, and, apparently, people have to go without food to make sure everyone has something to eat.

Granted, "it hurts" doesn't necessarily mean, "it's wrong." We permit dentists to prick our mouths with needles to fix our teeth. We let surgeons cut us open and move about our chest cavity to heal our hearts. Even free market policies, when activated to correct mistakes caused by big government, cause pain. We tolerate the doctor's pinch because it means we're eventually cured. Might we not tolerate socialism's brutality to heal our nation in the long run?

Maybe, if it meant fixing all our problems; we might permit the screams of socialism if socialism healed the nation. The problem is that it *doesn't.* Socialism doesn't make anything better; socialism makes everything worse. Tolerating its excruciating pain to "heal the country" is like tolerating a doctor who repeatedly and knowingly hurts you without curing your ailment. That's not healing; that's abuse.

Socialism's riddled with stories of starvation, isolation, despair, and madness. It promises many cures, but none of them are ever delivered. Anyone can listen to slick political-salesmen talk about utopian benefits, but in actual socialist nations, none of those benefits manifest.

However, in spite of all this overwhelming physical and logical evidence on the contrary, many people still utter the utterly nonsensical phrase, "Socialism's good in theory." Socialism's not good in theory. Socialism's not even a good theory. A theory's only good if it accurately models reality, which socialism doesn't, and a dogma's only good in theory if it leads to something righteous, which again, socialism doesn't. Thus, even though socialism can be forced upon a country, it *shouldn't* be forced upon a country. Even if it were logistically logical (which it isn't) to impose socialism upon a people, morally, it shouldn't be done. In order to understand why, let's start by properly defining what socialism is.

Socialism is a system of economics where private ownership doesn't exist. It begins by targeting factors of economic production. Businesses, factories, farms, and other wealth-producing industries are conquered by the state and transferred to the public [government].

But it doesn't stop there.

If socialism's truly the destruction of private ownership, families can't privately own their homes, workers can't privately own their cars, and most terrifyingly, individuals can't privately own their thoughts. It drops a guillotine on free speech, opinion, belief, and intellectualism, because every personal thought is a private thought, and every private thought is a form of private ownership that must be eradicated.

Because socialism means private ownership does not exist, socialism means property rights do not exist. No socialist can truly say, "this is mine," because any other man can say, "this is mine, too!" "Thou shall not steal" no longer has meaning, because stealing implies taking something that isn't yours, but in a socialist nation, everything's yours.

Thus, every act of self-defence becomes an act of assault. Every act of defending your property becomes an act of denying someone else's right to their property. There is no such thing as trespassing, because everyone owns all the land in the country, and the man who shoots a stranger breaking into his home commits murder, because there's no such thing as "one's home."

Ask any socialist why he's opposed to capitalism, and he says it's because of greed, labour exploitation, and the fact that one or two big businessmen decide how much of a particular good to produce. But then why would such a man want to be a socialist? If his contention with free-market capitalism is that it oppresses others by giving businessmen too much power, why would he adopt socialism as his economic crusade? After all, socialism's nothing more than the purported evils of capitalism taken to their extremes.

Activists argue capitalists exploit people for cheap labour, but socialism exploits people for *free* labour. In capitalist nations, cruel business owners exist, but workers can freely leave their jobs to search for better bosses. In socialist nations, cruel business owners also exist, but workers *can't* leave their jobs to search for better bosses, because there's only one boss: the government. Finally, crony capitalism means monopoly multiplies, and one company decides how much of a particular good to produce. But socialism means monopoly also exists, and only one company—the government—decides how much of *every single* good to produce.

In this, socialists aren't just monopolists; they're supreme monopolists. To demonstrate this reality more clearly, think about a sandwich.

One of life's greatest and most divine pleasures is a lunch in the middle of a hard-day's work. Wealthy men and women eat caviar like luxurious kings and queens for supper, but I pity they've never enjoyed a fresh, soft, sandwich, with salted chips, crisp vegetables, and an ice-cold bottle of water, while physically working outside on a hot-summer's day.

There are few things so satisfactory, both for the stomach and soul, as munching on a stacked architecture of thinly-shaved black forest ham, two slices of cold American cheese, a generous amount of bright yellow mustard and white mayo, crisp iceberg lettuce that's shredded, and dill pickles, all neatly assembled between two triangle slices of soft white supermarket bread.

Complimented with the crunch of thinly-cut chips and the snap of orange carrots, all washed down with a brisk bottle of water fresh from the fridge, a sandwich is one of man's greatest inventions and achievements. It's also one of socialism's greatest failures.

A variety of ingredients are needed to construct a sandwich. People get all their groceries from grocery stores, but that produce has to come from somewhere. That means travelling to a farm. Some farmers grow hard-red spring wheat, and other farmers grow corn. Ranchers raise pigs and cattle, and orchards grow peaches and apples. Through the miracle of modern markets, all of those products are inspected, packaged, refined, and delivered to our homes for consumption.

We do not think often enough about how profound this market-system is. The fact that we can buy bananas, cream of coconut, and rye bread, at the same time is a luxury that previous generations never comprehended. We choose what we want to eat, and farmers compete to capture a slice of the market.

They do so by offering the lowest costs possible, while also maintaining high standards of quality. If the price of their product jumps too much, or if the quality of their good decreases too much, people switch to a different supplier, maintaining equilibrium. But what if, instead of millions of farmers producing crop, only *one* farmer controls the means of *all* agricultural production in the continent? He is agriculture's perfect monopolist, and he wields incredible power.

He lays claim to tremendous assets, chief among them being fertile land, both in the north, where the climate's conducive for growing cereal grains, and in the south, where the climate allows fresh fruits to flourish. Of course, land alone isn't sufficient to plant and harvest crops, so this monopolist farmer also controls all the magnificent, multi-million-dollar machinery, needed to do so. The semi-trucks, grain trailers, 4-wheel-drive tractors, augers, grain carts, combines, and sprayers, are incredible, and complicated. They're assembled using metal, plastic, silicone, and an almost innumerable number of moving pieces and gadgets, and those parts don't make themselves.

To consolidate his monopoly and ensure he truly owns all the means of agricultural production in the continent, our lone farmer controls the mines, smelting plants, and factories, that forge and assemble his critical components of equipment.

If already this sounds too complicated for any one man to handle, that's the point. And remember, the farmer still has to plan for storage, processing, selling, and shipping of the harvested crops. That means the farmer not only owns all the agricultural land, seed, and machinery for his enterprise, but also all the grain elevators, storage barns, and refrigerators.

Wheat's milled into flour, so the farmer owns all the mills. Canola's crushed into oil, so the farmer owns all the crushers. Pigs are cleaned, so the farmer owns all the butchers, and so on.

Speaking of pigs, enough food for one is like finding enough money for a politician; it's an impossible task. The more you give them, the more they want. Butchering is just as difficult. A butcher's work is an astonishing art. They're precise and efficient surgeons. The fact that no one thinks about them when considering skilled jobs tells us just how impressive their proficiency with a blade is.

In a free market, butchers compete with each other to waste as little meat as possible, offer quality cuts, and present a delectable looking consortium of meats. In a monopolist market, where one farmer owns all the butchers, all of that competition disappears. It doesn't really matter how nice the cuts are, because people don't have other buying options. As such, who cares whether the butcher is skilled, or not? Why would the farmer waste money on paying expensive butchers, when he can hire cheap ones and sell his pork (no matter how ugly) for the same price?

From this short, oversimplified, example, two truths are immediately apparent. First, it's logistically absurd for one man to be a true monopolist and own *every single* factor of production in his business. Returning to farming, rational men recognize that it's impractical for any one man to own and control all the means of agricultural production.

I'm not saying farmers are foolish or incompetent. Both my parents came from the farm. I worked on a farm. I know that farming is a difficult job. Many men specialize in one thing, but farmers specialize in almost everything. While certain people specialize in accounting, and others in chemistry, the farmer's both an accountant, and a chemist. In the morning he tests his soil for nitrogen; in the evening, he tests his costs and futures contracts for profits. Other men are truck drivers or foremen, but the farmer is a foreman from the cab of his semi, giving orders to his hired hands while unloading grain at a bin by himself.

All of that is difficult enough for a farmer when he only farms barley, oats, and wheat. How much more difficult would his task be if he also farmed canola, rye, bananas, oranges, cotton, corn, apples, peaches, and sugar? By itself, that's an illogical enterprise, but it becomes so much more illogical when we factor owning, building, and controlling, mines, factories, forges, assembly lines, butchers, trains, and grocery stores into this convoluted equation.

The second truth is that if the monopolist owns everything, the quality of his product seriously suffers. A lack of competition means he doesn't have an economic reason to keep the quality of his product high. Whether he spends $10 on quality, or $7, the price at which he sells the good to us remains the same.

It's important to note I didn't use the word "impossible" in the previous few paragraphs. I didn't say it's *impossible* for any one man to own and control all the means of agricultural production, but rather, it's *impractical* for any one man to own and control all the means of agricultural production. I didn't say a single farmer (or organization) controlling all the means of agricultural production is an "impossible enterprise," but rather, an "illogical enterprise."

Granted, while I'm not comfortable saying it's "impossible" for a farmer to own all the means of agricultural production, I am comfortable to say it's impossible for him to do so *efficiently.* No mortal possesses the capacity to control every aspect of agriculture, while also producing value-maximizing outcomes. This is true for not only agriculture, but all other markets as well. The monopolist might strike it rich, but the rest of the people suffer from a lack of competition, and therefore, a lack of quality, choice, and competitive prices.

Herein lies an economic revelation. Everyone, the socialist most of all, knows it's pure madness to have a monopolist control every factor of economic production. And yet, *that's precisely what socialism is.*

Socialism means the government has total control of all factors of production in an economy. Whether a single farmer owns all the farms, machinery, and grocery stores in a nation, or a demagogue does, what's the difference?

The difference is that if a farmer controls the agricultural sector, ideologues call him an evil, capitalist, monopolist; if a bureaucrat controls the agricultural sector, ideologues call him a generous statesman.

If a single farmer controls the entirety of the agricultural sector, our dream sandwich will resemble something more like a nightmare. Think about how much worse it is for a bureaucrat, who probably knows nothing about farming, to take the farmer's place. It's happened in history before. For those states that demand control of grain, land, and output, the consequences are haunting. The socialist experiment has failed, washed away by the blood of hundreds of millions who died to prove what regular men already knew.

People often ask, "If it's so obvious that socialism doesn't work, why do activists try to force it on our nation? If it's so obvious that socialism's an economic wrecking ball, why do bureaucrats try to wield it?"

The answer lies within the question.

We might as well ask, "If bombs cause so much destruction, why are some countries dropping bombs on other countries?" The only answer is that warring nations want to destroy each other. Likewise, *progressives* use socialism to achieve their hideous aims. Progressivism is not socialism, but progressives use socialism like a tool. They unleash a devastating socialism because they want to devastate western society. They seek to rule us with an iron progressivism, but because it's so illogical and insane, society doesn't willingly capitulate to their ideology. Men do not naturally say that 2+2=5, or that man can be woman, like progressives want them to.

Thus, because people don't believe in progressivism willingly, they're made to do so *unwillingly*.

True, progressives can mobilize a military, and force progressivism upon us with marshal law, but why would they do so, when they have the near-omnipotent power of economic superiority at their fingertips? What if those same men who refused to say that "2+2=5" or "man can be woman," discover their families are in danger of starving? What if a man comes home every night, empty-handed, to malnourished children hoping for provision? The inability to provide for oneself, let alone for one's family, is a more painful injury than anything a military weapon can inflict.

All our leaders have to do is hold out a loaf of bread to fathers and say, "Here. Take this meal. It's yours. All you have to do is utter the code, 'males can be females, and females can be males.' All you have to do is repeat what we believe. That's not so difficult, is it?'"

If this scenario sounds far-fetched, it shouldn't. It's easier and more politically-fashionable to stand up to a tank than it is to Trotsky. Normal men won't march in a pride parade, but they might very well do so if it means their children don't starve. No one dares bite the hand that feeds him; what about the hand that feeds, clothes, houses, and heals everyone?

If government controls a nation's supply of bread and food, and if marching in a pride parade is a requirement to obtain that food, many men will bite the bullet and walk down the streets, clad with false rainbows and pride, to ensure their families don't go hungry.

If government owned every house in a city, as they do in socialist cities, a bureaucrat might come to one's door, and demand, "Say man is woman, or lose your government-provided home and freeze in the cold streets!"

Remember the lockdowns?

Many Canadians held out, and refused to be vaccinated for COVID-19, until they couldn't visit their favourite restaurants. They were living, but they weren't allowed to live. Children couldn't play their favourite sports, fathers couldn't enjoy cigars with their friends, mothers couldn't chat in coffee shops, and Canadians couldn't enjoy Canada. Grappling with forsaken income, strained mental health, and worsening emotional distress, countless millions felt forced to surrender to government's commands, and they did what they never wanted to do.

To take another example, remember Canada's trucker convoy? The people's democratic roar was overwhelming. Canadians wanted their freedoms back, and they were protesting peacefully, but seriously, in Ottawa.

Beaten, in an unbridled fit of rage and fury, government froze protestors' and convoy supporters' bank accounts. In an instant, every Canadian became very quiet. For many, all their money was gone. All their cash was stored in their accounts. They needed (and still need) access to their funds to pay bills, buy groceries, and provide for their families. How could they do so if government locked them out of their vaults? Government, by taking immediate control of people's economic situation, took immediate control of their lives.

Clearly, socialism is a dangerous weapon. It's a battle-axe, that, although imprecise, is heavy, and terribly effective. The more socialist our leaders are, the more economic control they exercise over us; the more economic control they exercise over us, the more power they exercise over our families. Their ideology's undeniably cruel, but for some reason, socialists act like they're compassionate.

The problem with socialism isn't that it's good, but that it's far too good. There's something even more dangerous than hating all the virtues, and that's loving one particular virtue far too much. Just ask the victims of a leader with a zealous lust for perfection. A virtue that's isolated from all the other virtues goes hideously mad, and turns into something monstrously unvirtuous.

Take the virtue of courage, for example. It's an excellent thing that men should be courageous, but without humility, their courage is poisoned by the putrid sin of pride, and they become unbearable brutes. Or, courage that goes forth without mercy means men conquer vast swaths of land, but they leave none of the innocents alive.

Progressives, using socialism, suffer from the same sort of problem. They have a variety of objectives, doing what's right in one's own eyes being chief amongst all, but they also strive for *equality.* Woe unto the nation that perfectly achieves it.

There's really only one time when all men are perfectly equal, and that's when they're perfectly dead. No matter, progressives take it upon themselves to ensure the society we live in achieves a more pronounced equality than anything we've seen before. No one disagrees that it's virtuous to treat everyone, whether king or janitor, equally, because all of us are made in the image of God. Slavery is an abomination because it treats humans as less than human. We are all infinitely and equally valuable, and no mortal is more worthy of our worship than another. But the problem with the progressive vision of equality is that, by disregarding all other virtues, they turn the virtue of equality into the equal suffering of poverty and misery. They take their desire for equality entirely too far.

Intellectually, some human beings are smarter than others. There's nothing inherently wrong with this, but because it means everyone isn't perfectly equal *in every way,* progressives impose intellectually-based affirmative action in school. Doing so discriminates against brilliant students, and treats them like they're no smarter than average workers.

Naturally, men are physically stronger than women, which means men are naturally better at sports. Again, this is unequal, so progressives demand co-ed leagues, neglecting the fact that the physical capacities of the genders are entirely different.

Economically, socialism steals and redistributes wealth, because everyone needs to be "financially equal." The idea that some men earn more than others is intolerable for ideologues, so they purchase (or conquer) every business, factory, and piece of private property, in the name of eradicating private wealth. “If everyone can’t be equally rich,” says the socialist, “then I will make all of them equally poor.”

All the while, progressivism continues to advance. Using socialism, they inject their ideology into the deepest recesses of our homes. Big bureaucracy cares more about how high our fences are than they do for actual criminals roaming the streets. They pay more attention to how close garden sheds are to each other than they do the violent marauder who just looted a store. We’re approaching a reality where government tells us how to manicure our yards, mandating the number of coniferous and deciduous trees we have to display. Considering they’re telling us how to decorate the outside of our homes, it’s not unreasonable to say they’ll soon be telling us how to decorate the inside of our homes. If we can’t have fences taller than two meters, why should we be allowed to have dinner tables taller than a meter and a half?

Now we need permits to build patios; next, we’ll need permits to paint our bedroom walls yellow. Eventually, though, we won’t need a permit for anything, because government will simply decorate our homes as they please to avoid any potential violations. Everyone will be safe; everyone will be equal; everyone will be exactly the same.

The cardinal sin of socialism is that it destroys individuality. Progressives tell all of us to do what’s right in our own eyes, but in their march for power, they act like everyone has the same eyes, with the same desires, and the same goals in life.

We should be free to create things, including our homes and yards, in the image of ourselves. Doing so is an expression of our humanity as beings made in the image of God. As a child takes on the attributes of his father, so we take on the attributes of our Father in Heaven, part of which means creating what we like, when we like, with the materials we have.

Let me build a fence on my property where I want. Let me, as a farmer, put grain bins where I know they're supposed to go. Let me plant a garden with whatever vegetables I choose. Let me design a house and yard that fits my personality. Let me express myself in accordance with morality and law. I'm only free to do so if at first I have property to call my own.

I might not be able to paint like Rembrandt, but I can paint my fence with the colour that I choose. My home, my yard, my property, it's exactly that—mine. Man is servant to everything everywhere else. He serves his bosses at work, police officers on the road, and politicians in the court, but in his home, he is the king of his own castle. He is the artist of his world and chief designer of his country, manicuring his yard as he wants, and displaying it with righteous pride for everyone else, including the Lord, to see.

In this, it's not wrong to say, "This is my own. I want to do what I will with it." That's the nature of man. God made us that way. The commandment isn't, "Thou shall not own property," but rather, "Thou shall not take the property of someone else." Private property is a good thing. It's ingrained in our human DNA. Not even the socialists can escape it, for they're nothing more than greedy progressives who take capitalism too far. They bemoan their hatred of monopoly, but they're the most powerful advocates for monopoly in our time.

When they take control of property and production, they don't produce goods and services for millions of different individuals, but for *one* individual. They don't meet the needs of every person, for *one* person – the citizen.

They reduce all men to one man, and all women to one woman, and treat everyone exactly the same, as if they have identical tastes, preferences, desires, and needs. They treat humanity, not like a species composed of billions of individual humans, but as one homogenous unit, without diverse interests, utilities, or values.

That's why socialists preach equality so loudly. They have to do so in order to promote the idea that we are all really one person. The irony is unmistakable. By adopting socialism as their preferred economic apparatus, progressives shoot themselves in the heart. They believe in an ideology of perpetual change, but socialism ensures nothing ever changes.

Progressives act like the fact that socialism encourages equality is reason enough to impose socialism in our nation. But like Lewis said, "From propositions about fact alone no practical conclusion can ever be drawn."[6] It's one thing to say, "Fertilizer increases wheat output;" it's another thing entirely to say, "Therefore, we *must* add fertilizer to our crops." Maybe we should do so, maybe we shouldn't, but the proposition that "Fertilizer increases wheat yield" isn't sufficient to automatically conclude that fertilizer should be added to wheat fields.

A man could say, "Riding a bike makes you less likely to be hit by another car," but that doesn't mean government should simply take away everyone's cars. A panel of experts might recommend taking control of everyone's business to slow the spread of a virus, but that doesn't give government the right to confiscate people's property. Imposing socialism might increase equality, but that doesn't mean socialism must be imposed. If that's the case; think of all the damage we can inflict:

---

[6] Lewis, *The Abolition of Man*, 31.

We can make men perfectly safe from outside assault; all we have to do is lock them in solitary confinement. We can make men perfectly safe from food-borne illness; all we'd have to do is stop feeding them. We can make the nation stop emitting carbon dioxide; all we'd have to stop letting men breathe. As a matter of fact, we can make all men perfectly equal. We *can* achieve the socialist dream. All we have to do is offer everyone a piece of fruit from the leaves of a forbidden tree.

CHAPTER 4

The Kingdom of Law

We've all heard that religious men are "fools" who do not think. The truth is, if there is no God, men cannot think. The deadly danger with human thought is that it easily convinces itself to stop thinking. That's exactly what's happening in our universities, and other institutions in society. Today, academics are so "logical" that they're using logic to question logic; they might as well use mathematics to disprove mathematics. The vaunted halls of higher learning ought to decorate their walls with the ouroboros, for the venerated philosophers who lecture there are like snakes eating their own tails.

Tragically, these thinkers are doomed to the same fate as Mr. J.R.R. Tolkien's Ungoliant, who, possessing such a ravenous hunger to feed, consumes herself in *The Silmarillion.* Similarly, our intellectuals have such an insatiable desire to question everything in the name of reason, they use their reason to question the legitimacy of reason. They chop off their noses to smell them; they cut out their tongues to taste the muscle. They use their logic to justify what's entirely illogical. They are the destroyers of faith, yet conveniently forget that reason is a matter of faith.

We take it on trust that reason guides us to truth. After all, if reason is all there is, there's no reason to suppose it yields truth. Why should it? Why not instead assume that reason leads to evolution, socialism, or extinction? Thus, radicals using reason to "prove" God is dead, faith is a lie, and religion is wrong, meet a daunting paradox. Because they claim religion is wrong, or false, they must believe the absence of religion is right, or true. But again, on what grounds do they believe that reason leads to truth? And even if reason leads to truth, there's nothing that says we must assume that truth is good. It's one thing to say religion's a lie; it's another thing entirely to say that lying is wrong. The latter assumption doesn't follow from the former. For that matter, without some a supreme standard of morality that measures right and wrong, what does "wrong" even mean?

For moderns who do what's right in their own eyes, "wrong" means whatever they want it to mean. They believe that by escaping the constricting religious chains of their youth, they're finally free to think, when in fact, the only thing they're finally free from is thinking.

Nevertheless, they attack religion like it doesn't have any honest purpose, and argue the only reason for its existence is enabling a powerful few to blind the multitude to reality. According to these moral trailblazers, it's the religious, traditional, conservatives who are radicals, precisely because they're realists. They're called extremists because they legally demonstrate their rights at a peaceful protest and convoy; they're abnormal because they refuse to engage in abnormality.

In this, for those of us who are religious, "wrong" doesn't mean whatever we want it to mean; wrong means whatever God wants it to mean. Unfortunately, progressive psychoanalysis shows the foolish victims of religion, like Isaac Newton, Leonhard Euler, Carl Gauss, Blaise Pascal, Thomas Jefferson, and countless others who believe in the Divinity are brainwashed, hoodwinked, and swindled by greedy mystics and sages.

Granted, we take all of these accusations with a grain of salt, because they're produced from the mouths of men who argue it's ridiculous to believe everything came from something, but not ridiculous to believe everything came from nothing. They claim it's absurd to say an automobile-engine spontaneously tunes itself without a mechanic, but it's not absurd to claim the universe spontaneously tunes itself without a Creator. Everyone knows that houses don't design themselves (that's why we have interior designers), but we're supposed to believe our galactic house, the universe, designed itself. We can't call a line "crooked" unless we have a definition of "straight," but it's said we can call a criminal "crooked" without appealing to a standard definition of morality. It's no wonder these modernists are so confident in their thinking; they don't believe in a supreme mind, so they don't have any intellectual standard to compare their thoughts (or lack of them) to.

Reinforcing their argument that religious men don't think, modern men cite religion's historical appetite for suppressing free thought. Now, no one disagrees that's sometimes, even oftentimes, the regrettable case. But the opposite is also true. As industriously as some devious religious men work to hide truth, there are other, equally industrious, religious men working to unveil the truth. Some ministers preach the ugly reality about their religion's past, while other ministers try to hide it. The Catholic church restricted translations of the Bible to common English, but Tyndale said, "I will make a boy that driveth the plough know more of the Scripture than the Pope," and translated the Bible for everyone to read. A powerful sect of religious bureaucrats in Judea martyred a peculiar carpenter preaching what he called, "The Gospel." They thought they buried their bane underground, only to frightfully discover a fearful fact about truth; one can bend it, twist it, crush it, and mock it as they choose, but its bones will never crack. One can even crucify the Truth on a cross, but it simply rises from the dead to live once again.

Neither can we forget that while certain religious leaders and zealots have a hideous history of hiding truth, non-religious leaders and organizations have a terrible history of doing the same. There are religious men who ban reading Bibles, but there are also non-religious men who ban Bibles. The Romans killed Christians in the name of religion, but Mao and Stalin killed hundreds of millions in the name of eradicating religion. For every monster who believes in God, there's another monster who doesn't believe in God. For every argument that says religion creates evil, there's a parallel argument that says the absence of religion does the same.

Whether it's religious, or non-religious men committing evil, both groups feel their actions are justified. The religious men feel justified because they believe their God is on their side. The non-religious men feel justified because they don't have a God telling them they're wrong. While progressives do what's right in their own eyes, most, if not all religions include a set of moral instructions telling their followers how to act. It's these very instructions progressives complain are patriarchally restrictive, and intolerably oppressive. We call these documents "objective codes" because they're the inarguable, unquestionable beginning and final commands that tell members of a particular belief what to do.

Of course, different religions command different things. Buddhists are vegetarian, but Hellenists eat meat. Christians are told to "love your neighbour as yourself," while Hindu's believe in loving your neighbour because he is yourself. Jews know they're supposed to worship YAHWEH; Muslims know they must worship Allah.

The correctness, or incorrectness, of each particular religious code is not yet of consequence. It's true that each code is mutually exclusive, but for the moment, that doesn't matter. What matters right now is that such codes exist. For a Christian, the Bible is that code; for a Muslim, it's the Koran. They're the objective measures of morality in the eyes of their followers. For each religious group, actions are deemed "right" if they adhere to their particular objective code, and actions are deemed "wrong" if they disobey the code.

Without such codes, objective judgements are impossible. A student can't fail his essay unless there's a rubric. Different teachers have different rubrics, but all of them have rubrics. A company can't "hit emissions targets," unless there's a target. Different countries have different targets, but all of them have targets. A sports player can't take a penalty in a game, unless there's a rulebook telling him what actions are impermissible. Different sports have different rules, but all of them have rules.

While rubrics, targets, or penalties, are different from situation to situation, the foundation of rules across all examples is generally the same. Students aren't allowed to cheat on their exams, spouses aren't allowed to cheat on each other, and companies aren't allowed to cheat on their accounting. For children, that looks like keeping your eyes on your paper; for spouses, it means keeping eyes on each other; for accountants, it means letting government keep their eyes on you. While cheating in school, the home, and the business world look different, neither students, spouses, nor workers, are permitted to cheat.

In this, while religions can vary wildly in their conduct, they do not vary wildly in the foundations of their conduct. There's a code beneath the objective codes. Mr. C.S. Lewis calls this "code beneath the codes" the Mandarin label, *The Tao.* Others call it *Natural* Law. Paul calls it "*a law unto themselves* [the Gentiles]" (Romans 2:14). For the rest of this chapter, we'll just call them the *Values.*

To better understand this code beneath the codes, take the increasingly prevalent example of suicide. The Christian scriptures forbid suicide, and call it dishonourable, so Christians live. But the Bushido code calls suicide honourable, so Samurais commit seppuku, and die. By their physical actions, the two religions are diametrically opposed, but their appeal to honour is exactly the same. While Samurais commit suicide, and Christians actively avoid it, both religions invoke honour to justify their actions. If suicide, or not committing suicide, is the action, honour is the justification.

To take another example, think about an invasion in the middle of a holy war. Invaded and invader alike fight to defend, or conquer, a section of land. Though their beliefs contradict each other, soldiers on both sides fight in the name of magnificent courage. Traits like loyalty, strength, and posterity, are the reason they fight. While combatants believe in different gods, both of them believe in bravery.

Thus, there are foundational *Values* like courage, humility, honour, and kindness, and there are actions that physically display those values. Religions disagree, and often disagree very violently, about how to exemplify the *Values*, but they generally don't disagree about the *Values*, themselves. The physical manifestation of the *Values* like justice, loyalty, charity, love, and perfection, look different from religion to religion, but the foundational *Values* are common to religions, precisely because they're common to mankind.

In this, it's one thing to argue a particular religion's method of materializing the *Values* is wrong, and a different religion's way of doing so is right. Everyone, religious or not, argues about that all the time. Both Christians and Stoics believe in justice, but as a Christian, I believe the Stoic's vision of justice is incorrect, and incomplete. We don't argue about the fact that justice must be achieved, but rather, what achieving justice looks like.

To take a more extreme example, think about cleanliness. Ordinary men think cleanliness looks like a spotless house, while perverted autocrats think it looks like eradicating an Abrahamic people from the face of Earth. No one argues that cleanliness should be realized; people argue about what realizing it means. For this reason, progressives can't call anything truly "right" or "wrong." They don't have an objective rulebook telling them how to play the game of life, so nothing is truly evil, or impermissible. They can't call murderers "bad" any more than they can call heroic veterans "good," because the words, "good or bad, cruel or merciful, just or unjust" all invoke the concept of a universal standard of morality—the very thing progressives are trying to destroy.

The repercussions of their unbelief are devastating. It means they can't call Hitler and his atrocities objectively sinister. They can't rule Stalin's Ukrainian genocide absolutely reprehensible. They can't call assault of an elderly woman vile, or the desecration of a grave inexcusable. All possible objective truths about reality, positive or not, are forsaken for a misguided belief in subjectivism.

However, while it's one thing to argue about how to exercise the *Values*, it's another thing entirely to argue about the *Values*. It's not radical to argue someone's version of justice is wrong, but it *is* radical to argue that justice is wrong. In fact, it's logically impossible do so, because to argue justice is wrong, one has to appeal to a standard of justice that says justice is unjust.

Likewise, it's entirely reasonable to argue about how to manifest honour, but it's entirely unreasonable to argue about whether honour should be manifested. If a man tries to do so, he appeals to a sense of honour, for even if he believes in doing what's dishonorable, he must think it honourable to be dishonorable. He can't say it's dishonourable to be dishonourable, otherwise, he agrees with everyone else who says it's honourable to be honourable. But if, according to this man, it's honourable to be dishonourable, why is he promoting dishonour? In his worldview, doing so is the honourable, and, therefore, the wrong, thing to do.

The devastation that occurs as a consequence of questioning the origin of the *Values* is a complicated, but critical point to understand. Remember the Christian and the Samurai. The Christian's code says committing suicide is *dis*honourable. The Samurai's code says committing suicide *is* honourable. The two religions argue back and forth about whether or not suicide's an honourable thing, but they never argue about the value of honour, itself.

As for the progressive, he can't attack, or reinforce, arguments regarding the demonstration of honour because he has nothing objective upon which to stand. Any appeal to right or wrong is an appeal to an objective code, and any appeal to an objective code is an appeal to something other than progressivism. If he argues that suicide's dishonorable, the Samurai easily counters with, "Based on what? You say suicide's wrong, but you're a subjectivist. Both of us are equal human beings, so who are you to tell me I'm misguided in my particular belief?" Or, if he argues that suicide is honourable, the Christian, as easily as the Samurai, says, "Based on what? You say suicide's right, but you're a subjectivist. Who are you to say I'm wrong in my belief that suicide's dishonourable?"

Out of options, the progressive moves from questioning *how* to demonstrate the *Values,* to *why* we ought to demonstrate the *Values*. Religious men, and even tepid agnostics, easily answer very quickly with, "We ought to pursue the *Values*, like chivalry, because chivalry is *good*." As a matter of fact, the common denominator of *all* the *Values*, whether charity, honour, love, peace, joy, or loyalty, is not only that they're good, but that they're goodness, itself.

The *Values* aren't good in the same way that a chocolate bar is good to eat, or a baseball game is good to play. Chocolate bars are good to eat *because* they're sweet, and stimulate joy by promoting the release of endorphins. Baseball's a good game to play *because* it promotes comradery, teamwork, loyalty, and physical health. Things like chocolate or baseball have reasons for their goodness, but the *Values* are the reasons. The *Values* aren't good because they promote diversity, or guarantee socialist equality; they're good because they *are*. There's no need to justify the *Values*, because the *Values* are the justification.

We don't give a reason for trying to be honourable; honour is the reason. It's not, "I'm working hard at my job, so I'm trying to be honourable." Rather, it's, "I'm trying to be honourable, so I'm working hard at my job." Likewise, we don't give a reason for expressing chivalry, because chivalry is the reason. It's not, "I'm going to give up my life, so I want to be chivalrous." Instead, it's, "I want to be chivalrous, so I'm going to give up my life."

At this point, progressives are welcome to ask why goodness, and not something else like feminism, ought to be the foundation of the *Values*. If they're successful in changing our minds, they can change the *Values* to fit their vision of the world. We adopt chivalry because we say that chivalry's good, but if progressives convince us that we should pursue values reflecting feminism, instead of goodness, we might be persuaded to disregard chivalry, and replace it with equality. So, why not adhere to a different code of values, grounded in something beyond goodness, like science, or progress?

Again, the answer is simple. We have to ground the *Values* in goodness, because there isn't another choice. Every attempt to justify the *Values* on some grounds other than goodness, like comfort, safety, or feminism, leads to an infinite regress of absurdity.

For example, if progressives base the *Values* in progressivism, all we reply is, "Yes, but why should anyone be progressive? Why should it be progressivism and not conservativism we adopt as our standard of value?"

All attempts to manoeuverer around the word "good" are vain. The progressive can say his value system rooted in progress is necessary because it's, "effective, feminist, and equitable," but doing so means he must answer the questions, "Why should we be effective? Why should we be feminist? Why should be strive for an equitable society?" Feeble explanations are no use. If the man appeals to the fairness of equitable living, or the innovation of the effective world, we once again return to those stubborn questions like, "Why should we be fair? Why should we innovate?"

Even the scientist, daring to base his values in chemistry or biology, encounters this dreadful problem. All we ask in return is, "Yes, but why should we ground morality in what scientific papers tell us? Why should we obey the science, and not the arts?" Even if the scientist counters with the convicting argument, "Because the science is true," we merely reply, "Perhaps, but why should we follow truth?"

The only way to stop this eternal descent into madness is to at once and forever agree, as everyone intuitively knows, that the *Values,* and the inherent goodness of the *Values,* cannot be questioned. In the case that progressives try to do so, trading the *Values'* foundation of goodness for something like feminism, we ask on what grounds we should appeal to feminism. The arguments that feminism is, "equal, modern, and tolerant," are countered with, "Why should we be "equal, modern, and tolerant?" Eventually, progressives must capitulate and admit they believe in a foundation like feminism because they believe that feminism's good. When they inevitably say it's good because it promotes equal treatment, kindness, and respect, we simply answer that those reasons are merely part of the same *Values* they're trying to eradicate.

At this point, we have to deal with a moral juggernaut. All people admit that certain states of values are pure goodness, but what, or *who*, determines what goodness is? If there are so many disagreements about how to demonstrate the *Values,* like justice, why aren't there disagreements about the *Values*, like whether justice should be demonstrated? We've already answered that we have to pursue the *Values* because we have no other choice, but who determines whether the *Values* are objectively good or not, and what gives them the right to do so?

Once again, it's not difficult for religious men and women to answer this question. Their God, whoever that might be, is their standard of right and wrong. He's their square that defines what "straight" means, and the level that demonstrates what the plumbline of morality is.

The pitiful Euthyphro gives an approximation of the same answer before being intellectually thrashed by Socrates. When the mighty philosopher asks Euthyphro, "Is something right because God commands it, or does God command it because it is right?" Euthyphro collapses and retreats without a satisfactory response. Many moderns invoke that same dilemma against religious men, today. However, the dilemma's unintimidating and unimpressive because it *isn't* a dilemma. A thing isn't good because God commands it, and God doesn't command something because it's good, but rather, **something is good because God *is* the Good.** A thing is good because *He Is.* The *Values* of justice, honour, kindness, compassion, mercy, and charity are all constituents of God's nature, and because His nature is the definition of goodness, the *Values* are goodness, too.

All of this isn't to admit every religion is true. That can't be the case. As a matter of fact, all of them must be false, except for one. We grant the fact without hesitation that an almost innumerable amount of sacred religious texts exist in the world, and all of them order different things. Different religions have different gods, and different gods command their followers to obey different rules. Embedded in those commands are statements so cutting and divisive, they demand exclusion. Even the progressive attempt at reconciliation between tradition and modernism that says, "All religions are true in some way," is really the statement that all religions are false in every way because all of them preach that only their religion is correct. As it turns out, preaching an inclusive gospel means preaching an exclusive gospel.

Before discussing which god is true, and, therefore, which religion is true, the fact remains that progressives aren't ruled by any god. They can't base morality in the Divine because they don't believe in Him, and it means obeying an objective standard of morality.

But while progressives refuse to believe in God, they do believe in themselves. Non-progressives who ask, "Who is the giver of morality and value?" look up to the Heavens and shout to God, "You are!" But when progressives ask the same question, they steal a sacred phrase from the Sovereign Supreme in Heaven, and answer with the blasphemous phrase, "*I am.*"

On its own, idolatry is reprehensible enough. It's dangerous for anyone to do what's right in their own eyes, because doing so, by definition, means doing what's wrong in the eyes of God. But it's made even more terrifying by the fact that so many progressives conquer political power. They finally accept that the *Values* are goodness, but not before usurping God's throne, and making it their own. They are no longer the servants of goodness; they are the source of it, and rather than obeying the *Values,* become the generators of it.

It's no wonder they crave power. As much as radicals want to do whatever they feel like, they're still restricted by civil and criminal law. There are limits on their actions in public life, even if there aren't any limits on their actions in their private lives. However, politicians repeatedly prove their irritating ability to shield themselves from the full prosecution of the court. They stumble in corruption, but nothing ever comes of it. All of us do evil, but politicians do evil without facing the wrath of the common citizen's court.

Lord Acton famously said, "Power tends to corrupt. Absolute power corrupts absolutely." We generally accept that Lord Acton is right, but Lord Acton is wrong. Power doesn't corrupt man; power merely amplifies man's inherent corruption. It enables the corruption already present in leaders to manifest in a more unrestricted manner than what's otherwise possible.

If it were true that power corrupts men and women, what would fathers and mothers be if not demagogical tyrants in their homes? After all, they exercise absolute power inside their kingdom's walls. What are they behind their front door if not absolutely powerful?

More than that, if it were true that power corrupts people, why do we find that children are already so corrupted? Everyone who's raised kids remembers toddlers lashing out or kicking and screaming in defiance. For that matter, we remember engaging in such actions ourselves. Even *without* any power at all, before bodies rumble with a hunger to rule, while still subject to the will of our parents, the spirit of rebellion (or "corruption" if you please) is already in man.

Though we still have corrupted desires (just look at your neighbor's internet search history, provided he's allowed to look at yours), the law restricts the physical manifestation of that corruption. Obviously, that restriction's a very good thing. But those who assume the thrones of political office don't just evade the restriction of law; they *become the law*. They use their newfound power to pass laws in government permitting whatever they believe is right, which often means legalizing what's wrong.

In this, we ought to reject the idea that young men and women who strive to be mighty politicians are best suited for the job. We're wiser to fear the 15-year-old with massive political aspirations than we are to cheer him on. Those who want power most are those who should have it the least. Those who crave power first are those who deserve it last. Mr. Tolkien properly said, "The most improper job of any man, even saints (who at any rate were at least unwilling to take it on), is bossing other men. Not one in a million is fit for it, and least of all those who seek the opportunity."[7] The regrettable fact about our democracy, though Mr. Churchill rightfully called it, "the worst form of government, except for all the others that have been tried from time to time," is that to acquire power, one has to crave it, and actively seek it out."[8]

However, there's a shimmer of hope. Not every legislator is so naïve as to think themselves uncorrupted before acquiring power. There is another breed of politician, one progressives hate the most, who, in rare instances, are burdened with the heavy cross of righteous power. He's the man who doesn't want power. He's the man who knows how dangerous power is. He's the man who wants to rule for as short a time as possible, and then retire to a quiet life beyond the public eye. He's the opposite of everything hungry politicians are, which is why he's perfect for the job.

---

[7] Mark J. Perry, "Quotation of the Day on the Most Improper Job," American Enterprise Institute, May 23, 2015, https://www.aei.org/carpe-diem/quotation-of-the-day-on-the-most-improper-job/.

[8] International Churchill Society, "The Worst Form of Government," February 25, 2016, https://winstonchurchill.org/resources/quotes/the-worst-form-of-government/.

Such men are platinum, for they're even rarer than gold. Progressives who want power, however, are like rust, abundant and invasive. Baptized with rulership, political progressives devolve into little gods, see themselves as the source of goodness, and falsely generate new values for mankind. Thus, chivalry is traded for equality, cleanliness is traded for filth, charity's traded for selfishness, truth's traded for lies, and life is traded for death.

The physical examples of these new "values" in society are manifest. We're supposed to fight for life, but our leaders promote death (they're only able to do so because they're alive) through maximum euthanasia, abortion, and safe-injection sites for drug addicts.

In the case of cleanliness, we used to promote clean cities and power. Now, our leaders promote putrid streets riddled with dangerous individuals and homeless camps. Oil, gas, and nuclear power are clean forms of energy promoting clean cities and countries. But our leaders demand we switch to solar and wind power, made with rare earth metals, that poison foreign victims unfortunate enough to live near the vicinity of a mine.

Finally, there's the matter of chivalry and equality. Women used to be venerated in society, but thanks to the modern demand for equality, all of that's gone away. The left claims they want absolute equality because they love females and femininity, but they don't. They hate females; they hate femininity.

Progressives parade around the streets cheering that the apparent age of masculinity is over. And yet, at the same time, they work their hardest to become masculine. They complain how terribly men oppress them, and have oppressed them historically, while at the same time, gleefully demand that women compete with men in sports. They hate to be dominated by men, but they're happy when their sports are dominated by men.

A little while ago, I heard that a new female powerlifting record was set in my country of Canada. I looked it up for myself. I didn't read about any female record being set. I read about someone lifting a lot of weight, 597.5 pounds in fact, in a female powerlifting competition, but the person doing so wasn't a woman.

Clearly, progressives rule the Earth, and they've flipped our world upside down. They erect a kingdom of values and laws that defiantly reject the *Values* and laws of God. They make it seem like their enlightened way of life is progressive and innovative, but it's really nothing new. What they're doing has been done a thousand times before.

For example, once upon a time, two brothers—a farmer and a shepherd—lived with their family in a Mesopotamian oasis. The young men, trained in the knowledge and wisdom of God, matured, and did what was right in the eyes of the Almighty, until one day, the eldest brother rebelled, and did what was right in the eyes of himself. As he offered up his sacrifices, his spirit of sacrilege, pride, and anger, produced a profane stench in Heaven, and his offerings were rightfully rejected by the Divinity.

During the older brother's madness, he saw his righteous younger brother's sacrifice eagerly accepted by God. The farmer's jealously grew into an unbridled monster. It made him happy to be angry. He loved to hate, felt perfectly sane in his insanity, and, feeding his fury, armed himself with a stone, and beat his younger brother to death. He felt peace in the middle of his rage; he felt alive the moment he took his brother's life.

Exiled for his hideous sin, the brother left his oasis, and travelled into the wilderness. He didn't repent, but rebelled, and entrenched himself in sin. Wandering as a nomad, he eventually settled, and built a city, expanding into an empire of the abject hatred of truth, justice, love, peace, salvation, and Almighty God.

We know the names of these two brothers, and we tremble as we realize the murderous son's empire never fell. It's assumed different forms throughout the millennia, but it's foundational principle of "doing what's right in one's own eyes" remains unchanged. Our progressive leaders work their hardest to fortify this kingdom, and barricade all of us inside its city walls. Ruled by lawlessness, and protected from the compassionate love of God, all of us live in the Kingdom of Cain.

CHAPTER 5

The Kingdom of the Cross

By now, it's obvious we have an insurmountable problem. Millenia of progressivism have taken us exactly where we don't want to go. We've done what's right in our own eyes in hopes of a better life that's full of freedom, but instead, it's led to is a life that's saturated with depression, war, worry, and death. All we have to do is look at the state of our world to see that it's true.

Wanting to escape progressivism, a man turns into a recluse and takes himself out of the world, only to fearfully discover he cannot take the world out of himself. Even if he hates progressivism, he still finds himself doing right in his own eyes all the time. He builds magnificent temples to protect himself from the evils of the Earth, only to realize he *is* the evil of the Earth. As fast as he tries to outrun progressivism, he tries to outrun his legs. All of us working to escape the Kingdom of Cain slowly understand it's impossible to do so. We can't flee from its modern influence because there's nowhere left to run. Every square inch of the world's been conquered by progressivism, precisely because every square inch of the world's been conquered by mankind.

Even if, by miracle, we discover a location that's free from progressivism, the moment we claim it in the name of ourselves is the moment it's mutilated by progressivism's murderous brush. It doesn't matter if we summit the Himalayas, or paddle to the beaches of remote Madagascar; wherever we go, progressivism comes with us. We can't hide, or run, from our problems, because *we* are the problem.

We might compare our present condition to men infected with smallpox. Of course, there are a few cruel monsters who love to spread it around. They drive from town-to-town, infecting everyone else with their disease, simply because they have an evil desire to do so. But there are other, earnest men who are infected, as well. They see their neighbours succumbing to the mindless virus, and try to escape its deadly fate. In bids to save themselves, they run away as fast as they can, ignorantly seeking refuge in nearby cities. Of course, when they arrive, it's not like they're saved from the disease; rather, they spread the disease to everyone else. Their physical symptoms are not yet manifest, but the virus ravaging their bodies still passes from person to person. Tragically, their eager hope for salvation turns into a desperate realization of horror as they watch everyone around them fall to the plague they unintentionally delivered.

But even elementary doctors know that if a host dies, the virus dies. It follows that one of the possible ways to defeat progressivism is to extinguish its host. If the human race goes extinct, so does progressivism. If we exterminate our species, progressivism has nothing left to cling to, and it disintegrates into dust. The obvious problem is that this tactic means massacring mankind, which gives progressivism exactly what it desires. After all, the death of mankind is the ultimate objective of progressivism. Everything it encourages us to do, from rejecting our natural biology, to telling us to stop thinking, incurs the destruction of our race. If we kill ourselves to kill progressivism, we don't vanquish our enemy, but lose to it, and our apparent victory turns out to be eternal defeat.

Thus, we can't free ourselves from progressivism, because all of us are guilty of doing what's right in our own eyes. And, we can't commit genocide against our species, because that means progressivism's victory, so what are we going to do? There's nothing we can do. In fact, the question isn't, "What are we going to do?", but rather, "What is someone going to do for us?" Because we can't save ourselves from progressivism, we need a Saviour, one who isn't progressive, or compromised by our progressive nature, to do it for us. Just who, exactly, is that Saviour going to be? We all believe in different religions and gods, so which religion and god is true?

When we collectively envision humanity's Messiah (we can also call him *The Christ*), we think about more than just a regular man; we think about a superman. In our eyes, Messiah must be mankind's perfect specimen in every way. Granted, different ages have different versions of what perfection looks like, but the principles of perfection remain the same. He must be beautiful, with perfect physical symmetry, defined features, strong characteristics, and a muscular structure like Adonis. He must surpass Gauss, Newton, and Euler in the classroom, while dominating Napoleon, Hannibal, and Alexander the Great on the battlefield. He needs to bring peace to the world, convincing everyone to live in harmony through his unchallenged prowess in negotiation and oratory. With an intellect eclipsing Einstein's, statesmanship surpassing

Churchill's, strength outclassing Samson, and wisdom beyond Solomon, our expected Messiah is to be everything we desire. Then again, so many politicians promise to be everything we desire as well.

It's surreal to observe man's blind infatuation with men. We exhibit a foolish fascination with political leaders, and act like they're going to save us from all our problems. Inevitably, with each batch of hopeful new demagogues comes renewed promises for our nation, even though the Teacher of Ecclesiastics (Ecclesiastics 1:9-10) says, *"What has been is what will be, and what has been done is what will be done, and there is nothing new under the sun. Is there a thing of which it is said, 'See, this is new'? It has been already in the ages before us."*

Nothing ever changes, but for some reason, as fresh politicians ascend to their iron-clad thrones, we think that things are going to change. It's shocking that we put our faith in them. Doing so is like a pile of dirty dishes placing faith in one particularly charismatic dirty dish to save all of them from their mess. Countless billions put their hope in worldly leaders, which is probably why the older many of us get, the more hopeless we tend to become.

The clearest proof that our politicians aren't our saviours from progressivism, aside from the fact that the overwhelming majority of them are progressive, is that like us, they're subject to the shackles of the grave. Mr. Charles Spurgeon said, "Six feet of dirt make all men equal,"[9] and our political leaders aren't exempt from that fact. Powerful tyrants in the ancient world are powerless skeletons in the modern one. They've met the

[9] Charles Haddon Spurgeon, "Charles Haddon Spurgeon Quotes," Good Reads, https://www.goodreads.com/quotes/432012-six-feet-of-dirt-make-all-men-equal. Accessed Jan 2, 2024.

same fate as their victims. No one presently fears Stalin because Stalin's buried in the Earth. No one fears Caesar because Caesar's decaying underground. The conquerors of history who once trampled dirt are now the dirt that new conquerors trample on.

The fact of death for everyone is so certain and plain that not even our political leaders attempt to deceive us about it. Mr. Justin Trudeau or Mrs. Kamala Harris say wild and wicked things, promising to save us from our problems, but never once do we hear them proclaim, "*I am the way, and the truth, and the life.*"

Other leaders promise grand economic reforms, or a flood of social programs, but none of them so much as utter the phrase, *"I am the resurrection and the life. Whoever believes in me, though he die, yet shall he live, and everyone who lives and believes in me shall never die."*

But there is one Man who dares to authoritatively say such things, and He's the last person we'd ever expect to do so. He's the one who alone causes the Earth to quake, armies to tremble, and the most powerful forces in the cosmos to reverence at the mere mention of His name, *Jesus Christ.*

It's strictly unbelievable that a peculiar little carpenter from Nazareth claims to be mankind's Messiah. He's everything opposite of what we expect Messiah to be. He's not a powerful statesman; He's a humble tradesman who's driven out of His state by a mad ruler. The only army He commands is a dozen rough fisherman and their misfit entourage of oddballs and outcasts. He doesn't have a face all of us are attracted to, but rather, one that makes all of us consciously force ourselves to look away. He doesn't seem powerful, but powerless, and is subject to the heavy empire of the Julio-Claudian dynasty. This "mystic" carpenter of Judea doesn't have the strength of Samson, the harmonies of David, the military of Moses, or the political influence of Daniel. Instead, He's clumsy, strange, and forgettable. As much as this man named Jesus claims to be the Christ who saves us from our problems and progressivism, it looks far more like He's Anti-Christ.

Then again, what if Jesus only looks like Anti-Christ because our perceived vision of who the Christ is, and what He's supposed to be, is manifestly wrong? Suppose a colony of eight billion brown ants, living underground, is constantly harassed by their archnemesis, the mighty anteater. It's inconceivable that the brown ants expect a red ant to be their saviour from the enemy. In fact, it's probable that the brown ants kill the red ant upon his arrival, falsely assuming he's an invader, not a saviour, in their blind misunderstanding of who their Messiah must be.

Likewise, it's absurd to think a progressive society conceives of an anti-progressive saviour. If we create our perfect Christ, we create Anti-Christ, because we're the cause of our current mess. If we want to escape progressivism, the last thing we want is a saviour who's welcomed by the Kingdom of Cain. We shouldn't be concerned if our Messiah is hated by the world; we *should* be concerned if our Messiah conforms to the world. A leader who is loved by the world is a leader who loves the world. But a leader who loves the world isn't one who can save us from the problems of the world.

Of course, the fact that Jesus is radically different than our expectation of Messiah isn't sufficient to conclude He's Messiah. If the only pre-requisite to be a saviour is to be the opposite of what we think a saviour should be, cowards turn into heroes, and weak men turn into strong ones. Similarly, if the only requirement to be a christ is to be a tradesman, or carpenter, millions of christs are walking all around us, every day. Almost all of these tradesmen are humble and generous, but they're certainly not messiahs, and to their honourable credit, they're the last ones to claim that they are.

Clearly, there must be something different about Jesus of Nazareth. If a homeless carpenter, walking around the countryside, claiming to be the fulfillment of prophecy appeared today, we wouldn't dare put our faith in him, so why do Christians put their faith in Christ? Why are an increasing number of people proclaiming that Jesus is the Christ, Messiah, and Saviour of mankind? Almost everyone looks at His teachings and readily admits He was an excellent teacher, but Dr. Richard Feynman, and Socrates were excellent teachers too. It's evident that Jesus felt compassion for the poor, but many of us also feel compassion for the poor. His miracles were extraordinary among men, but there are magicians, like those in Pharaoh's court, who performed miracles as well. None of these actors, though they share similar traits with Christ, are messiahs, so why does the title fall to Jesus?

More than that, it's not like Christ is the only religious leader in the world. Muslims appeal to Mohammed, and Buddhists look to Siddhartha Gautama. Greeks worship a polytheistic religion, Russian atheists serve the state, and progressives worship themselves. Every religious, or anti-religious, group claims supremacy over the others. Because they make cutting and conflicting claims, only one belief can be objectively true. What gives Christians the right to say it's theirs?

If we want to do so, we can test the truth of every minute detail in every religion, but that takes an intolerably long time (longer than we have to live), and it's horribly inefficient. There are a massive 10,000+ recognized belief systems in the world.

Trying to discern which one out the 10,000 is absolutely true is like finding an honest politician in parliament. It's almost impossible to do so, and testing every command, statement, and pledge guarantees frustration.

Instead, it's much more effective to triage. Rather than investigating millions of tedious claims, let's investigate one massive claim. After all, we do it all the time. Rather than looking at every single house when house hunting, a couple efficiently eliminates thousands of choices by telling their realtor they only want a bungalow. Or, instead of test driving every car, a man narrows his options and tells the salesman he wants a half-ton pickup truck with the luxury package. By investigating the mutually exclusive claim of Christianity, we can effectively determine whether it's false, or not. If the claim is a lie, Christianity is a lie, and all other religions are up for investigation. But if the Christian claim is true, all other religions and beliefs in the world are, by definition, false. Only one step remains; what truth claim are we going to test?

When we look at all the religions, we see many extraordinary statements. When we observe the events of history, we see many unbelievable things. Napoleon crows himself Emperor, Caesar conquers the known world, Pharaoh builds geometric pyramids, and Babylon unveils intimidating ziggurats for the gods. But as mighty as those events are, all of them pale in comparison to the gravity of Easter morn over 2000 years ago. Reality hinges on a Man. Truth depends on the position of a stone. Life is won or lost in the darkness of a tomb. Christianity makes a claim that no one else makes, and no other religions accept. The belief of Christianity is the one event that dwarfs all other events, and it's the fulcrum of past, present, and future: *The Resurrection.*

The only explanation for the multitudes' belief in Jesus Christ is that they must be entirely convinced He's alive. And, considering it's uncontested, even among unbelievers, that Christ was real and died on a cross, Christians must believe that Jesus was raised from the dead. Remember, Christianity comes with a sword, for it distinguishes itself from all other beliefs by putting its faith in a man, and not in the ideals of a man. Marxists believe in Marxism because they do not believe in Marx, but in the writings of Marx. Atheists believe in Atheism because they don't put their faith in Hitchens, Hume, and Voltaire, but in the writings of Hitchens, Hume, and Voltaire. In a fit of panic, feverish disciples of Alexander the Great or Hannibal might pray to their commanders while they're alive, but not anymore. Because these great generals are dead, no one expects Alexander to save them, and no one hopes for Hannibal's second coming over the peak of a mountain pass. Only Christ claims to live. If He's dead, Christianity dies.

In this, The Resurrection matters because it satisfies all disagreements in our world. For example, Christ isn't the only one who says, "I am the Truth." The Muslim mystic, Al-Ḥallāj, infamously says it, too. Or, like Jesus, the Pharaohs believe they're divine. And, while Christ proclaims, "No one comes to the Father, except through me," modern progressives claim, "There is no Father, only me." But if Christ is raised from the dead, Christianity is true, everything Christ says is true, and all other religions, including progressivism, are false. It's the final and perfect proof of Christs' claims. His resurrection means Al-Ḥallāj *is not* the truth, Pharaohs aren't divine, and there is a Father in Heaven. A summary of the Christian story will help us see why this is the case.

Countless religions existed by the age of Herod the Great. Caesar Tiberius ruled the world. Sacred texts and beliefs battled for supremacy among the people, and there was no Messiah to be found. The Jewish God, YAHWEH, was mute. However, in the middle of this silence, the 30-year-old Jesus of Nazareth started preaching around the land of Galilei. He chose what we now call "The Old Testament" from among all other religious texts, and started teaching that all of it was perfectly true. He affirmed the Ten commandments, repeated the prophets, and asserted the legitimacy of Jewish law, but He didn't stop there. Beyond merely approving the law, Jesus started preaching He was the fulfillment of the law. He never said He was an agent of God; He said He *was* God. He didn't just admit the prophecies concerning a promised Messiah; He claimed to *be* the promised Messiah. The Scriptures spoke about a prophesied saviour, and Christ said the Scriptures were talking about Him.

When one reads the entirety of Jesus' life on Earth, it's easy to see why progressives hated Him then, and why they continue to hate Him now. He represents everything they despise. The humble preacher is the complete inversion of everything progressives envision in a leader because He affirms the objective law and rejects the idea of doing what's right in one's own eyes. The progressives of Jesus' day said the same thing they say today, "You can do it, you are enough, you can help yourself," but Christ told them to repent, countering their idea that "you can help yourself" with the Scriptural teaching, "You cannot help yourself; you need Me." As religious leaders told the people man could work their way to God, Christ told them He *was* God, and didn't just work His way to man, but *became* one.

Of course, Christs' exact words are recorded in the Bible, but in the interests of brevity, we'll only paraphrase what He says. In short, He teaches that the Jewish Scriptures are absolutely true. He tells the people to follow the commandments, for the commandments are good. He tells them to stop doing what was right in their own eyes, for doing what's right in one's own eyes is evil. He calls every word of the Scriptures accurate, correct, and divinely inspired. Only His death and resurrection can show the world He's right.

Jesus is clear. He says the same Old Testament Scriptures He calls perfectly correct (insinuating the incorrectness of every other religious text), are the ones that speak about Him as being the Messiah of the world. According to Jesus, the same Scriptures He calls holy and true are the ones that call Him the prophesied Saviour of mankind. Perhaps the most explicit example of this radical claim occurs in Luke 22:37 where Jesus says, *"For I tell you that this Scripture must be fulfilled in me: 'And he was numbered with the transgressors.' For what is written about me has its fulfillment.*"

Here, Christ is saying, "I *am* the suffering servant the prophet Isaiah spoke about. I am the Saviour of man who will be wounded, beaten, pierced by a spear, chastised, punished by God, judged, and slaughtered like an innocent lamb to rescue our species, just as the Scriptures say. But not only so, again, just as the Scriptures prophesy, I *will* be raised from the dead, three days after my crucifixion, and live eternally. This is who the Scriptures say man's Saviour will be, and this is what the Scriptures say He will have to endure, and I AM He."

Christ said the Old Testament was true. He said the Old Testament's prophecies about our Saviour, including dying on a cross and being raised to life on the third day, were true. He claimed to be that very Saviour. There was only one thing left for Christ to do: **prove it**. If He wanted to prove He was the Saviour of mankind, He first needed to die, in order that He could be raised to life. The human race, marred by its progressive madness, and hungry for righteous blood, was happy to oblige.

For progressives, everything lined up perfectly. Their nemesis—the One who preached doing what was right in the eyes of God instead of doing what was right in the eyes of oneself—was betrayed by one of His disciples, captured by the Romans, and handed over to the Jewish Sanhedrin to be judged for His Messianic claim. After being sentenced with blasphemy and condemned to die, Christ was mocked, tortured, traded for a murderer, humiliated, and forced to labour His heavy cross up the hill called Golgotha. There, Roman soldiers drove nails into His hands and feet, and crucified Him in utter indifference. The Lord Jesus Christ suffered in agony for hours, slowly suffocating until the crescendo of history came to pass in the middle of the afternoon.

Finally, His objective complete and His mission fulfilled, the Carpenter from Nazareth surrendered His spirit, gave out a powerful cry, breathed His last, and died. Our supposed Saviour from progressivism, preaching to stop doing what was right in our eyes, was killed by those who did what was right in their own. Surely this means progressivism prevailed and is superior to Christ.

That would be the case if progressives didn't walk directly into Christs' perfect trap, but they did. The moment they ruled over Jesus is the moment they became His unknowing servants. As they killed this perfect person on the cross, they ensured eternal life for people. Our disobedience of the Scriptures, killing a man who didn't deserve to die, and rejecting God's supernatural servant, meant we obeyed what the Scriptures wrote about us, and Christ. By disregarding the prophets, we fulfilled the prophecies of unbelief and betrayal they spoke about. Every time moderns belittled Jesus, rejected His Messianic claim, and called Him a fraud, only further proved the legitimacy of His title, for that's exactly what had to happen to the Messiah. Progressivism wins when it presides over the death of men, but it lost when it presided over the death of a Man. Its greatest victory is actually its mortal defeat. Let the "enlightened" members of our age tremble, for progressivism's triumph over Christ proves to be Christ's triumph over progressivism.

By the resurrection, Christ demonstrated He's everything He claimed to be. For example, take His charge that He was "Life." The death of Christ is the only way for Him to prove He's not just alive but *is Life.* It's not enough for Him to live, because all of us are living. It's not even enough for Jesus to live a long time, because he might merely have a protracted lifespan. Instead, in order for Jesus to prove that He was Life, He needed to partake in a sort of contradiction in terms. He could only demonstrate His superiority over death by going to the grave. A person who says, "No prison can detain me," must be locked in the strongest prison to see if it's true; a greater Man named Jesus who said "no grave can hold me" must be buried in a tomb, sealed by a mighty rock that thieves couldn't move to display that He was right. All men perish to show that they're sinners, but Christ perished to show that He was sinless. The only way He could prove He was Life was to first commit an unthinkable paradox, and die.

Or, what about Christs' claim that He was not just true, but *The Truth?* How else could He prove that except by the resurrection? Aristotle said that "To say of what is that it is not, or of what is not that it is, is false; while to say of what is that it is, or of what is not that it is not, is true."[10] This is called "Correspondence Theory," and a majority of philosophers agree it's the best definition of truth. A statement, for example, is true if it describes reality as it is, and a statement is false if it describes reality as it is not. This makes progressives very mad, because it means reality is independent of what we believe about reality. A man is still a man, even if he believes he's a woman. Reality doesn't obey men; men must obey reality.

But while reality doesn't obey men, it does obey a Man. Men are called "truthful" if they submit to reality, but Christ is called "The Truth" because reality submits to Him. The change is glaring. When we speak about reality, we do so from an angle of observation. This means we speak the truth. We say the sky is blue, not because we order the sky to adopt such a hue, but because it is. Or, we say that gravity causes objects to fall at a rate of 9.8 metres per second on Earth, not because we ordain the mechanics of physics, but because it is.

However, when Christ speaks about reality, He does so from an angle of command. This means He *is* the Truth. Christ says, "The tree is green," because that's the colour He wants the tree to be, and so it is. He said that blind men would see, and so they did, because that was what Christ wanted to happen. We understand the difference. A man says, "The sun will rise in three days," and knows he's speaking about structured reality. But when the Lord Jesus said, "The Son will rise in three days" and He was going to restructure reality.

[10] Stanford Encyclopedia of Philosophy, *The Correspondence Theory of Truth*, May 28, 2015, https://plato.stanford.edu/entries/truth-correspondence/.

We don't worship a dead Jesus, but a risen Jesus. We aren't the disciples of a mystic from the past, but of the King of the past, present, and future. Our Lord is Alpha and Omega, First and Last, God and Man, Servant and King, Lion and Lamb. He is the Truth, the Life, the Standard of Perfection, and the Measure of Right and Wrong.

Thus, in a stunning irony, we Christians who reject progressivism are the only ones able to actually progress. While progressives are running around frantically, like chickens with their heads cut off, we fix our eyes on Jesus, and move towards Him, precisely because He moves towards us.

If progressives really wanted to progress, they'd repent of their evil and turn to Christ for salvation. Unlike them, we're able to progress, because we have a living, unchangeable, standard of goodness named Jesus Christ, acting as our leader, measure, and guide. For if Christ is a changing God, it's impossible to progress, because it means altering the test of goodness, instead of passing it. If He changes from day to day, then what's right in one age is wrong in another, and the term "progress" dissolves into a word without meaning.

Think about it. Suppose men in the 1500s prefer to be ugly, while men in the 1900s prefer to be beautiful. We can't say one batch of men is progressing over another, because both groups are aiming for different targets. The men of the 1900s don't better conform to the standard of beauty than men of the 1500s, because the men in the 1500s weren't trying to be beautiful. If the standard changes, any hope of improvement, or *progress*, is destroyed.

In this, we don't defeat progressivism by stopping all progress. We defeat progressivism by progressing *properly.* Jesus Christ is the conqueror of the Kingdom of Cain. Without Him, there is no escape, and there is no salvation. There is only one name under Heaven by which all of us might be freed from our present condition, and it's Christ. He's man's only Saviour, and perfect Messiah. His strength is proven in His weakness on Earth, for only a supernatural man of the mightiest constitution could conceal His glory from us in the way Christ did. His compassion is proven in His sacrifice, for He didn't just die for those who loved Him, but for all of us who hated Him. Eternal life is promised for *anyone* who simply believes in the Lord Jesus for their salvation. This perfect gift from God isn't earned by our good works, it is a glorious gift of grace to be received by our faith in Christ. Heaven awaits, and the Lord is coming back very soon. Don't delay, says Paul, believe in Christ today, lest the opportunity pass over you, never to manifest again.

Let us heed a warning. It's appointed unto man once to die, and after this, the judgement. Purgatory doesn't exist. There are no second chances after death. If a man rejects God's salvation in this life, he will reject it in the next. The Lord will not demand those who hate Him to be with Him in Heaven. Rather, He will give them what they desire—an eternity in Hell separated from Christ. Once again, Mr. Spurgeon is potent when he says, "You are hanging over the mouth of Hell by a single thread, and that thread is breaking. Only a stopping of the heart for a single moment, and you will be in an eternal world without God, without hope, without forgiveness."[11]

If there's one thing we should preach to progressives, it's to open their eyes and believe in the Lord. I've always thought

[11] Charles H. Spurgeon, *A Clarion Call To Saints And Sinners*, The Spurgeon Center, April 2, 1981, https://www.spurgeon.org/resource-library/sermons/a-clarion-call-to-saints-and-sinners/#flipbook/. Accessed Jan 2, 2024.

it strange how they charge us Christians with the sin of being willfully blind. After all, progressives don't believe in Christ, so they don't believe in light. How is it possible, then, that they should see anything at all, considering they prefer to believe the cold and haunting noir of a galactic void is all that there is?

In a humorous sort of way, the only way to progress is to eventually stop progressing. A car that never stops driving launches itself over a cliff, but a car that stops driving enjoys the mountain views. The whole point of proper progress is to eventually arrive at perfection, so it's good that we fix our eyes on Jesus. But what happens if we progress beyond Him? It's no use trying to do so, for if we progress beyond Perfection Himself, we no longer progress. Thus, an entirely progressive world, where everyone does what's right in their own eyes, is a stagnant world. The modern progressive's mistake is the same as it's always been, and he discovers too late that to progress forever is the same as not to move.

Manufactured by Amazon.ca
Acheson, AB

13217929R00058